I0619920

When They We're Young

Steven A. Turner

Copyright © 2024 Steven A. Turner

ISBN (Hardback): 979-8-89381-029-5
ISBN (Paperback): 979-8-89381-028-8
ISBN (eBook): 979-8-89381-027-1

All rights reserved. No part of this book may be reproduced
or transmitted in any form or by any means, electronic or mechanical, including photocopying,
recording, or by any information storage and retrieval system, without permission
in writing from the copyright owner.
The views expressed in this work are solely those of the author and do not
necessarily reflect the views of the publisher, and the publisher hereby disclaims
any responsibility for them.

508 West 26th Street KEARNEY, NE 68848
402-819-3224
info@medialiteraryexcellence.com

Contents

Introduction

Gina has been sitting in her room for hours today. She can't tell you for how long because there isn't a clock in the room and at this point in her life, she can't tell you what she was doing ten minutes ago. Gina is 84 years old and lives in an assisted living home in San Jose California.

Her room has a nice comfortable queen size bed, a dresser with some of her folded clothes. There is a desk with a lamp and a chair in front of it, but she can't remember if she has used it. There is a closet full of her hanging clothes that easily slides open and closed. Unfortunately, Gina doesn't always get to choose what to wear each day.

The walls and ceiling are painted a light brown with bright white accents. On the walls are many pictures. Some days Gina can point to everyone in each picture and tell you who they are and where they live. Not today.

On the wall across from the window is a nice big screen television. She sometimes watches VCR tapes of family movies. They really make her very happy. Other times she doesn't know anyone in the movies.

This place that she lives in, washes her clothes and prepares her three meals each day. A very nice young lady walks Gina where ever she needs to go during the day. Don't ask Gina her name today, she just can't remember it. Janet is her name.

Gina has spent the last two years in this home. Before that she was a self-reliant lady. She had invested extremely well in the stock market and had built a very large portfolio. Gina, who was a breast cancer survivor, had organized the volunteer programs for cancer patients in the three main hospitals in San Jose and was also a volunteer helping with the patients. She had also spent time working for the United States Navy. Starting out as a secretary at the Navy base in San Bruno, Gina rose through the department to become the person in charge of the Archives Department on The Navy Base.

There are two pictures though that she always can tell anyone who the people are in those pictures. The first one is an 8 by 10 picture of the bust of Jesus Christ and the Sacred Heart. Gina prays to Jesus every night before she goes to bed. There are times she prays for hours because she keeps repeating her prayers.

The second picture is also an 8 by 10. This black and white picture is of Gina and her husband John. It was taken before they were married and when they were young. She spends most of her time thinking of John and when they were young. It was such a wonderful time in her life. She knows, in fact, that her 37 years of marriage to John were all wonderful.

Life really changed for Gina when John died of a heart attack at work. He was 62 she was 58. The year was 1977. The last 27 years of her life have been without the love of her life. What went on during that time? She can't remember much.

She often plays back in her mind how the two found each other and the stories of both John and Gina's lives. They both had very interesting stories that took place in San Francisco during the early 1920's and 30's.

Chapter One

It's a typical Wednesday morning on Evans Ave... You can hear the noise of the cattle rumbling down Innes Street from the stockyards on the hillside. They had arrived on Monday at midnight on the Southern Pacific Railroad by way of Topeka Kansas.

The Mexican vaqueros whistle and snap their ropes as the steers move at too slow of a pace for the riders. They need to get this lot of steers to James Allen's and Sons by 6:00 am and it's already 5:45. It usually takes thirty-five minutes to get all of the cattle too and in the holding pens, but this morning in the dark, a dog chasing a stray cat spooked the cattle and they got loose when the gates opened. With dust flying and the dogs barking, it took an extra fifteen minutes to calm them down and get them walking in the right direction.

 Jack Allen, who's father James, owned the largest slaughter house in "Butchertown", road up to Alex Manriquez on his eight-year-old large black bay horse. Jack was an average size middle aged man in his forties. He dressed in a flannel shirt covered by a jeans jacket and blue jeans over his legs. Big black cowboy boots were tight in the strips and a black bowler hat was on top his head. A red bandanna was tied around his neck that could be used when it was really dusty on the roads.

"Hey Alex! Ya gotta get this lot of cattle move en!! You're running late!! We need them by the start of the 6:15 kill!" Jack was not happy and Alex knew it.

"Se Senior Jack. No worries, we will get them there on time."

Alex galloped off up Newhall away from Third Street towards the oncoming heard just coming down Innes Street. All of the streets in Butchertown really were dirt passage ways. It didn't have any sidewalks and during the rainy times, they turned to mud. Today, with the morning due, the dust wasn't too bad. Alex was the foreman of the riders for Allens. He was very good at barking out orders and organizing his vaqueros. He was an excellent rider himself and he had been doing this since the rebuilding of the area after the 1906 earthquake and fire. This morning, he was far different than his usual laid-back self. The young riders who were spread out around the heard, could see by the look in his eyes, that he meant business. He sat low on his horse with his big round tan hat tilted to the side. Strapped around his waist was an old cowhide leather holster with his Colt 45. The new Colt had an oak handle with a raised horse on it. With his black and white bandanna pulled up over his nose and two gloved hands, one holding the rains of the horse and the other a small rope, he rode alongside of the heard so that he could get behind it. From there he and several of his boys began to smack their ropes to the sides of their horses and whistling to get the cattle moving down the street. Besides being the best vaquero around, he was also the best at settling arguments. No one knew if he had ever used his Colt and no one wanted to test him. He always had the final word and this morning he would make sure the heard was on time!

On this morning, the wind was blowing from the south off the bay. You could see the tress slightly bending and the leaves fluttering. It was cool but not cold. The fog over the bay had lifted with the breeze. Even with the breeze, the usual Butchertown smell was present. Those who lived there just got used to it. The breeze also meant that the rest of San Francisco would be able to "enjoy" the morning of an unpleasant day.

The men on Allens" kill floor", all twenty-five of them, had just finished with the morning's preparations for the morning beef kill. The cleanup crew of one, young Marv Bernhagen, was finishing washing down the new concrete floors into the waste chutes. Bernie was a 17-year-old with a thick German accent. He'd been working at Allen's since they reopened in 1907. Marv stood 5'8 and 190 pounds with a big barrel chest. He worked hard all day doing all of the heavy lifting and odd jobs along with keeping the place clean.

When they started the Beef kill process, and later in the day, the hog and lamb kills, all of the dead piglets from the large sows, blood, entrails and useless cuttings would be washed through the chutes and into the sewer. The sewer emptied out into Islais Creek about a half a mile away. The creek then emptied everything into the bay. This added to the unusual smell of the area.

After the 1906 earthquake, all of the slaughterhouses that were built above the creek had to be rebuilt on solid ground. Although the fire that followed the quake, didn't get to Butchertown, much of it was destroyed by the shaking of the April quake. All of the buildings fell into the creek when the piers crumbled. Twenty some places of work were built on the pier that was over the creek. Everything was moved inland when the rebuilding began.

"Hey Bernie – you awake this morning? Late night? Your move'en a little slow. Don't miss anything"
"Piss on you Federico! Ya dumb ass Dago! Your high-class whop relatives over in North Beach are sure as hell gone to smell us today". He said laughing.

Leo Federico is one of the butchers taking a break. As they sharpen their knives with their steels, and dressed in full length white gowns and rubber boots, they all grab a quick smoke. Most of the butchers smoked a quick cigarette on brakes. The self-rolled smokes would hang from their lips and bounce as they talked. They never used their hands to smoke, except to throw their butts on the floor. Not Leo though. He liked the big fat cigars. He could chew on them for hours and still got a little buzz.

Leo was the 31-year-old foreman of the killing crew. Jack and Dominic, his younger brothers were also part of the crew. They lived in Butchertown at the far end of Galvez closer to the bay. Leo had his own house with a family right next door to where his brothers lived with their parents.

Butchertown had a mixed ethnic population. Many Italians and emigrants from Malta, Germany and Ireland all worked at Allen's. There were some English and French emigrants too, but not many. Butchertown didn't have any African Americans at the time, but forty years later it would become all African American. You also had those who moved west from places like New York, Kentucky and Ohio the area also had many Chinese families who were shrimp farmers. The Bay at that time still had many opportunities for that type of business.

Behind the red glow of the cigar and a big puff of smoke, Leo used the hand signal of a full hand swiping under his chin twice followed by the old fist between his elbow and a great big laugh. All of the men who worked together really enjoyed the back and forth banter every day during their free time. When the work started though, they didn't have time for anything but work.

On days like today, the smell from the stockyards of wet cowhide, horses, horse droppings, dirty hogs and sheep, along with the smell from all fifteen of the slaughter houses and their corrals was normal. Add to that the pungent smell of the tallow companies and the stench of the rotted animal parts floating in Islais Creek, you had a definite character to "Butchertown". The widely ethnic cultures that lived there, were used to it. The rest of San Francisco and it's 1924 population hated it! So, when the wind blew like today, the Italian population in North Beach and Knob Hill, would get a strong whiff of "Butchertown".

Originally, all of the slaughter houses were located in "Little Italy" which was on the North end of town, along the edge of Chinatown and near the businesses of the Barbary Coast. When San Francisco first became a city, local government made a law in 1868, that prohibited the killing of animals in those certain parts of town.

The new area designated for this type of work, was several miles away in the marsh land full of stagnant ponds feed by streams from the rolling hills near Islais Creek, past Dog Patch and a mile east of Irish Hill. It became known as "Butchertown".

After the fire and quake of 1906, the method of processing animals slowly began to improve. By this day, Butchertown was down to fifteen different slaughter houses. At its largest, it had twenty-four. Most were located on the east side of Third Street, which was originally called Railroad Ave. After the quake, 26 streets running south to north were re-named alphabetically.

With the dust flying from Alex Manriquez and his horse, nine-year old's Johnny Turnbull and Little Joe Dalpagetto laughed.

"Alex is sure in a hurry. Must be late. Those vaqueros are going to be a hurt'en bunch if they ain't on time. Alex will beat all of their silly asses"

"Sure, as hell Little Joe. That's two days in a row. Mr. Allen likes everything on time. Some day you and I'll get to work for that guy. He works his guys hard but is fair and pays a great wage".

"Someday, but today we gotta work for your uncles. I'll be glad when those days come to an end"

"You got that right Little Joe. Working for my family ain't getting us anywhere".

Johnny and Little Joe have been best friends since they could walk. Joe's real name was Adolpho, but he hated it. Most kids called him "Little Joe" or just "Joe" because he was a real dark-skinned Italian who's parents immigrated from Sicily. He also had jet black curly hair, like the few young African American boys that lived in San Francisco. Little Joe was not a tall kid and would always be on the short side. He lived on Fairfax Ave. with his parents, brother Joseph, Big Joe, and sister Rose. He had been working at "Turnbulls Slaughter" for two years now. Johnny had helped him get work there when they needed an extra low paying worker. He was learning the trade and making very little money. What little money he made sure helped his parents. "Turnbulls" was the only place that would hire kids his age.

Johnny not John, started working at "Turnbulls" when he was six. His father and his brothers started the business in 1907. It was one of the smaller slaughter houses and it too was located on Evens Ave. two blocks down from Allen's.

Turnbull's was owned and ran by 51-year-old William Turnbull and his three brothers, Charles 44, George 31-, and 50-year-old Ed. Williams son Joseph, 20 and Ed's son Arthur 27 also worked as butchers and laborers at "Turnbulls". Johnny's father Robert or otherwise known as "Rock", worked with his brothers until he died of a heart attack in 1919 at the age of 50. Because"Turnbulls" was one of the smallest slaughter houses in Butchertown, they could not match the mass production of the other larger business's, so they did custom kills along with the normal butchering and would often go to people's houses or farms to do their work. They also did work for the small butcher shops around town. They did really well in Chinatown. Rock Turnbull was well known there when they started the business. He was always over there selling, delivering and working the shop owners.

Johnny's pay was below all other workers except his friend Little Joe. For every beef killed and butchered, Johnny received twenty-five cents. Hogs brought him ten cents and a nickel for every lamb. Even at nine years old, Johnny was the fastest and safest butcher in the shop. Everyone knew it and didn't like it or him, but he made them money. He was just like his Dad.

Johnny lived on Galvez Ave. in the upstairs apartment with an older woman of no relation who he called *"Ma"*. Others called her Aunt Lizzy. She had taken him into her home when he was ten months old. Aunt Lizzy was very tiny with a down home face. She was well known around Butcher town because of her outgoing personality and the different accent she spoke with. Kentucky is where she was from but her speech sounded like a girl from maybe Tennessee.

 Johnny wasn't really sure why he was living with Aunt Lizzy, but every once in a while, he'd pick up little bits of information. All he did know was that his older sister Margret, now 12, had lived with his Uncle Charles on Oakdale, with Charles's mother and sister Mary. He also knew that his real mother Lilly, died sometime before his first birthday and his father passed away after his third birthday. None of the Uncles or their families wanted anything to do with him, other than make him work. At nine years old, he didn't understand why, but he would someday find out. Until then, his feelings for his family were not very nice to say the least! Although he was family, he was not treated like it. The older cousins would always try to bully him.

He did love the hard work and all of his money went to help Lizzy and her other border, Rita. She was fifteen years older than Johnny and had been living upstairs in the same two-story house for twenty years. Lizzy took her in also after her parents died. Johnny and Rita, although not related were like brother and sister!

The rest of Joe's and Johnny's classmates were in school, which is where they should be. But, Bayview Elementary School and the fourth-grade classroom wasn't their favorite place to be! This

4

day would be spent looking for adventures.

"Let's head over to "The Corral" and check things out"

"Johnny, you going to ride that big ole black and white bay today, or is he going to buck you off again?" Little Joe loved to finish his jabs with a little giggle!

"Sure, why not! Let's race. Ready go!"

The Corral was located on Kirkwood. That's down Evans and up Fairfax three blocks. There was no chance of out running Joe head-to-head. Those short little legs could move faster than anyone in the neighborhood. The best way to beat him to the corral was over several fences and through some backyards. Only problem was avoiding several dogs that patrolled those yards.

Johnny finally cleared the last fence and had sprinted half way down Kirkwood when he saw Little Joe sitting on the fence to the corral. Giggling!

The corral was a place for guys and gals to go to practice and show off their rodeo skills. It had an arena and a track to race horses. There were always steers and sheep in the pens waiting to be slaughtered and none of the cowboys that worked there cared if they were used as targets for ropers or bull doggers. If anyone had a horse, they could be kept there in the barns. Especially the ones that were not broken yet.

"Got ya again, ya skinny little Irish Mick" again followed by that little giggle.

"I'd a beat you if that mean old hound in Williamson's backyard wasn't there. Dam near took a chunk out of my butt."

"Think I'll roll me a smoke before I find that painted hag ".

As Johnny lifted the papers and tobacco at Little Joe to ask if he was interested, several of the younger brothers of the vaqueros walked up behind Johnny. Joe tilted his head at Johnny to warn him something was up.

This group of kids aged seven to twelve didn't attend school. They worked part time doing odd jobs around the different neighborhoods until they were old enough to become vaqueros. The boys lived in "The Mission District" that was south east of Butcher town. The old Mission Deloris was located in the area, which gave it its name. Most of the population in that area was of Mexican decent. The boys would ride their horses over the hill that separated the two areas. Most of San Francisco was developing areas of the city based on ethnic back rounds and types of work that was done in that area.

The three boys encircled Little Joe and Johnny. It wasn't like these guys didn't know each other. They had gotten into it with each other before. The oldest, Gilberto didn't really like Johnny. They had a run in several weeks ago and things didn't turn out to well for Johnny. Gilberto reached down and picked up a small block of wood. He placed it on his shoulder and spoke.

"Turnbull, you boys man enough today? Or, are you just going to sit on that there fence? If so, get lost"

Little Joe giggled. He looked over at his best friend with a smile because he knew what the answer was going to be. Johnny smiled too. He put his papers and tobacco in his back pocket and stepped off the fence really slow. Continuing to smile he took three steps towards Gilberto, who stood about six inches taller and weighed twenty-five pounds more than Johnny. Knowing that as soon as he reached for that block of wood, things were on! And that was fine with Johnny. He loved guys with "a chip on their shoulder". It may have been his favorite thing to do, knocking blocks off. Back in this day that was how fights started and gave way to the expressions "knock his block off" or "the guy has a chip on his shoulder". This would be a good challenge he thought to himself, so let's do it!

Johnny quickly backhanded the wood chip off Gilberto's left shoulder with his right hand and blocked Gilberto's roundhouse right with his left forearm. Moment of truth now! How quick could he follow with his right before getting hit? Quick enough. Johnny landed his own right hand to the face of Gilberto under his left eye and a left to his nose! The first two punches surprised Gilberto but didn't have much effect on him. Because of his size advantage and Johnny's lack of power, the tide turned rather quickly. Gilberto smiled, then stepped into a hard right hand to the side of Johnny's face. It knocked him backwards into the fence. The noise from the tree boys watching and the thud from Johnny hitting the fence, got the attention of several of the cowboys that were nearby. The three cowboys ran to the scuffle and hopped over the fence to break things up.

Geno Dagostini grabbed Gilberto in a full nelson hold and picked him up off of his feet and turned him away from Johnny. "Little Willy" Chris Wilhelm went to Johnny, who was still on his feet, while old Brad Kudlac made sure the three other boys didn't get involved.

Kudlac spit his chew out and looked at the two boys *"what seems to be the problem guys?"*

Johnny had several cuts on his face, his shirt was torn and a few buttons were missing. Gilberto was sporting a bloody nose and a welt was developing under his left eye.

"This won't be the last time ass hole"

Gilberto said pointing at Johnny. He was really mad and the expression on his face was very telling. Although Gilberto definitely won the fight, he couldn't put Johnny down. The last fight they had, Gilberto dominated things and knocked Johnny down several times with punches to the face.

As Johnny smiled, you could see his two front teeth. They were not "bucked teeth", but they were large. His ears also were on the large side along with dark straight hair, almost a bowl cut. He wasn't a muscular kid, kinda on the skinny side.

"Fine with me Bert. I wasn't finished" Again, you could hear Little Joe's little giggle!

The older cowboys who broke things up made sure the two groups of boys went on their separate ways.
"Well at least you gotta couple good shots in this time" Joe chuckled.

"Working with Lefty sure helps! Those first two worked just like we practiced. And, he couldn't put me down." Turnbull said with a smile that hurt.

Now that playing at the corral for several hours was not an option, the two friends headed up to the hillside for a couple smokes and fun on a rope swing at the big oak tree. Then they could run after the sheep and goats that were grazing along the hill. The episode at the corral was definitely the high point of the day! Better than any reading or writing at school. But they still had to work at Turnbulls for a nine-hour shift later in the day. The good news was the weekend was just around the corner. After work Saturday morning they had the afternoon off and all of Sunday to have fun.

5:30 Saturday morning came slowly for Johnny. Wednesday, Thursday and Friday brought on some long hours of work to do along with going to school too. Aunt Lizzy got him up for bacon, eggs and some coffee. The youngster loved his coffee boiling hot and black.! No cream, no sugar! Always a great way to start the day. The walk to Turnbulls of five blocks would last long enough for a quick smoke. Today's nine-hour shift should go by fast. There shouldn't be a whole lot of different work to do, maybe they would go somewhere for a job. They all had spent the last three days killing and butchering only beef. The family had a large order to fill by Friday afternoon and they had to spend each day working longer than usual. It needed to get done and on time because business wasn't going well, and this was an important job.

The boys had big plans for Saturday and Sunday. On Saturday, starting at 4:00pm, the Bayview Theater was showing two movies for ten cents. Buster Keaton and Fatty Arbuckle were the stars of the first movie, a comedy called "Sherlock Jr." The second feature was an epic silent western called "Iron Horse". Sunday would be spent playing baseball after the 8:00 am mass at All Hollows Catholic Church on the corner of Paulou and Newhall. The first game was at noon at the Bayview Athletic Field on Jerrold Street. "The Butchertown Boys" had a nine-inning game with the guys from 32ed Street and after that they would play a group from Visitation Valley. Danny Carey and Kenney Miles who were at school last Wednesday and usually were with Johnny and Little Joe, would be along for the movies and the ball games.

Danny was two years younger than Johnny and Little Joe. He lived on Jerrold Street with his parents. They spoke French and some broken English. When Danny was a year old, he fell from the nearby train. Both of his hands were run over by the train leaving him with only thumbs on his hands. That didn't bother him much and he became very good at doing most of the same tasks as others. He looked up to the other three boys because they never made fun of him, let him tag along with them and they would always stand up for him against boys bigger and older than he. Danny was no easy mark anymore though. When he hit someone with those stubs, it really hurt!

Kenny lived one block south of Turnbull on Hudson. It was easy for Johnny to get to Mile's place. He just had to go out his back door, over a fence and into the Nixon's yard. They lived two doors down from the Miles on Hudson. Ken was the wise cracking, overweight fourth son of a family that had moved in from Texas after the earthquake and fire of 06.

These four typical "Butchertown Boys" had a lot of fun together and their friendships would last forever over the years. They would travel down the same roads together as young men and would always be at each others side when times became difficult.

The meeting place for the movies was always at Mooney's Candy and Ice Cream Parlor on Third and LaSalle. They had great milk shakes for two bits that would take half an hour to finish. From there, it was a five block walk up Third to the theater. Anytime there was a big double feature like today, "Big Dick" the local policeman would always be there. Mr. Otto, the owner of the Bayview Theater would also request that "Shorty the Cop" would also be along with "Big Dick". These two had a reputation of taking care of business in the neighborhood. Kids as well as adults didn't mess around with either. They were rough but always fair and honest. They also lived in the neighborhood.

The boys always made sure they had seats in the back of the theater, so that they could see who came in and where they sat.

"OH, OH OH. Look who's walking down the left side of the isles. It's the Turnbull girls; Marion and Johnny's' favorite sister, Margaret"

"That's all you're going to say Kenny. No wise cracks or else". At the same time as Turnbull spoke, he flicked Kenny's ear. "Ouch- asshole." Ken replied.

"Margaret, did you see who was sitting in the last row?"

"Yes Marion. And I'm sure that crude brother of mine and his hooligan friends will do something stupid again today. They are always getting into trouble."

"Well, I think that he is funny and his friends are too."

Margret Turnbull was Johnny's older sister by three years. They were split up years ago when their parents passed away. They also had an older sister that died at birth. Margret started out living with her Uncle William, then with Uncle Charlie and his older sister Mary Turnbull, but was now living with their Uncle George and his family. Marion was the only daughter of George and his wife May. Marion was born on the same day as Johnny, February 7 1915. Both Margret and Marion attended All Hallows Catholic School. Although they were brother and sister, Johnny and Margret didn't see much of each other and when they did, it was never friendly. For some reason, Margret had a very low opinion of her brother and he couldn't figure that out. Johnny considered his Uncle George and his son little George, who was ten, pains in the ass. Earlier in the year, Johnny knocked one of little George's teeth out when he called Johnny's mother "a crazy woman." He didn't understand that either, but Uncle George took a belt to Johnny and told him to keep his hands off little George. "You're just like your old man" He would say after the beating.

The first movie was just as advertised. Fatty Arbuckle was his usual self, with dumb comments throughout the movie. Kenny would have the one liner down by the end of the day and would use them for the next three weeks! Buster Keaton stole the show for everyone else. His stone-faced comedy had everyone laughing.
Margaret looked a lot like Johnny. You could tell they were brother and sister.
She was a tall girl and skinny just like Johnny. She never pulled her hair back in a ponytail. It was

always done up nice. It was a mix between black and brown. Glasses always covered her face along with freckles and a light skin color. Margaret, not Maggie or anything else always wore a nice dress and was very concerned about the way she looked. At school, she always received good grades!

Between movies, Marion walked up the isle to where the boys were sitting.

"Hey Turnbull I hear you guys are playing ball Sunday at the Bayview Field."

Marion had a crush on one of the players for Butchertown. Little Ducky Mahoney. He played second base and lived just around the corner from her house, on Newcomb. Ducky was four years older and went to Bayview Elementary. He was the typical Butchertown boy. He could always be found playing ball after school or a game of "kick the can". Duck was also a brawler. He had a bad temper and was always getting busy with others. In the summer, he and the rest of the boys would also hang out at the beach or over at the corral. Where ever "Big Dick" or "Shorty the Cop" were, they were not!

"Hi Marion. Yep, we start at noon and play two games. The 32ed Street boys and Visitation Valley guys are coming by for rematches from two weeks ago. You coming? If Uncle George lets you?"

"I would sure like too"

Marion was a pretty girl with long blonde hair and really deep blue eyes. She was tall for her age and you could tell she was going to be an even prettier young lady. Most boys thought she was really neat. Little Joe, Danny and Kenny got really quiet when she was around.

"'Well, if you do come, leave little George at home with my sister" They both had a good laugh at that.

"But if you need someone to go with, bring Nellie with you!" Johnny had a smile on his face.

Nellie Bloom was Marion's classmate at All Hallows. She was different than most girls at her school. On most days after school, Nellie would walk down to the corral. Nellie was very athletic and was the local Tom Boy. With her black hair in a bandanna, blue jeans rolled up a good four inches just like the boys, she could be seen racing her horse around the track or roping sheep in the arena. She was a shy girl around the boys, so she wasn't noticed much, but Johnny thought she was special. Nellie always had a pretty smile for Johnny.

"I'll try Johnny. It would be a fun way to spend this Sunday. I'll see Nellie on the way home"

Later, just as the Iron Horse was ending, everyone in the theater could hear from the back row a very loud "BURP, followed by a large laugh.

"I knew it. I knew it. He couldn't go the whole show without doing it"
Margret started to cry. Thinking that everyone was laughing at her because of what her younger brother had just done. Johnny Turnbull was famous around the neighborhood for his loud Burps!!

After Shorty and Big Dick ran the boys out, they all made their way together down Third Street towards home. They did make one quick stop at Cyril DeNikes place. Located at the corner of Galvez and Third, just a half a block from Johnny's house, it served the best stakes in the area and was the place to be if you were older than 20.

Kenny's oldest brother, Tex, worked there as a bartender. That excuse would get the boys into the backdoor of the kitchen. They just wanted to "see what was going on". Cyril was always in the bar area making sure things went smoothly. Although, he loved greeting the patrons of the restaurant, trouble didn't happen very often, but when it did, it happened in the bar.

"Turnbull- Little Joe! You two take Frenchy there and Miles out the back door! There isn't anything in here for you boys!"

Cyril liked the boys a lot. He knew they got into trouble all of the time, but it was honest fun. They never stole from anyone and they were good "Butchertown Boys".

Cyril used to work with Johnny's father, "The Rock". Rock Turnbull as he was known around Butchertown, used to run one of the "Hotels" on Irish Hill before he got married and opened up the slaughter house. Cyril was 15 at the time and he did many things at the "Monterey House". He stocked selves, changed kegs, washed glasses and cleared tables. He also ran errands for the dancing girls. It was always a busy place and fun to be at. When things were not fun and trouble began, The Rock became the law. Cyril learned a lot from Rock. And now he had his own place to run.

"Cyril! Need any help with the bad guys tonight? Need a keg changed?"

"John T!"

That's what Cyril called Johnny when he was serious and he knew he hated it!

"You need to go home to Aunt Lizzy tonight and get your chores done. Little Joe and Frenchy, beat it. And Miles, no food scrapes for you."

It was fun for the boys even if it only lasted a few minutes. They had a chance to watch the men and women dance and mingle in their fancy outfits. DeNikes was a classy establishment. Even though it was during prohibition, Big Dick and Shorty the Cop never came inside when they were on duty.

After going to 8:00 mass on Sunday morning with Aunt Lizzy and Rita, Johnny made sure he said hello to Mr. Allen and his son Jack. They and their family always went to 8:00 mass! The boys all met up at Bayview Field for the two games by 11:00. "The Butchertown Boys" had a pretty good team. Ducky Mahoney was like the manager while playing second base and leading off. Johnny played third base and hit eighth in the order. He wasn't fast like Little Joe, who played centerfield, but he would knock anything down that came his way. Neither Little Joe or Johnny hit as well as the others because they always worked and didn't have time to practice. Danny Carey, because of his hands didn't play, but he was there as bat boy, and went after foul balls and was a great fan.

Kenny was there too. He played backup catcher and watched!

All of the boys loved their baseball because of their hometown hero, Lefty O'Doul. Lefty grew up on Kirkwood and went to Bayview Elementary school as a kid. He was supposed to follow in his dad's footsteps as a butcher at Moffats Slaughter, but he found his way to the big leagues as a pitcher and first baseman. During the off season, he'd always be at the field on Jerrold Street pitching to the boys and hitting them balls. Once a year he'd drop by the house on Galvez to visit Lizzy while Johnny's sister Rita did his taxes. Lizzy was somehow related to Lefty, and he always made sure she was taken care of.

Lefty took a liken to Johnny. He also knew Johnny's father. The Rock had always been nice to Lefty. He actually showed Lefty how to box. The kids in Butchertown were a pretty rough group and got into it with each other all the time. Lefty had a reputation in pro baseball as a guy you really didn't want to get mad. Not only did he swing a bat and throw a baseball left-handed, he had a great straight left! Lefty would give Johnny pointers all of the time at the house and on the fields.

"Always keep your chin down. Hands up. Block with the same side hand. Always throw two punches. Never one"

Then they would spar.

Marion showed up just before the first game started with the 32ed street kids. Nellie was along also, which made Johnny very excited. He sure hoped he played well. He wanted to impress Nellie and just as important, win. The 32ed Street team had some older boys and, in the past, usually beat Butchertown. Games were played hard and tempers could get hot. But not today. 32ed won a close one 5 to 4 in a well-played game and everyone had fun.

In between games Johnny and Ducky went over to the bleachers to talk with the two girls. Johnny and Nellie hit it off pretty good. They talked about her horse and "stuff" that went on at the corral. After about fifteen minutes the girls had to leave. The four of them said good bye and smiled.

"That's a pretty nice girl, that Marion. Does it bug you that we are sweet on each other?"

"Na. Just treat her right! I know you can kick my ass, but she is my family. That piece of shit brother won't stand up to you, but you know I would"

"I know you would Turnbull. But I would never hurt her. You kinda sweet on Nellie?" Ducky asked

"For a girl she's alright! She can do most things guys can and better!" Johnny replied.

The whole time Johnny was talking with Nellie and Ducky, he kept thinking how much of a bad time the boys were going to give him. But he really didn't care! She was fun to talk to. None of the girls at his school gave him much attention. She was pretty and all, but he liked the way she acted. Not prissy. Nellie and her horse could out race everyone at the corral. And rope too.
The gang from Visitation Valley was done warming up and were ready to play. Danny came

running over to Ducky and Johnny.

"Ducky, their manager is ready to get started and he wants to go over some of the ground rules"

As Ducky stood up, he yelled thru the backstop *"Wally . Ross, I'll be right there"* Wally Ross was the manager of Visitation Valley.

Because these guys organized the games on their own, they didn't have umpires. The two managers had to agree on all of the calls. The team that was in the field would always be responsible for out and safe calls along with balls and strikes. If there was ever a disagreement, Ducky would do all the talking for Butchertown. The first game went well because there were not any close calls. Hopefully this would turn out the same way. Most arguments were solved with the bat toss, but those few that didn't get solved, usually ended the game with some pushing and shoving and maybe a punch or two! If that was the case, the Butchertown Boys were always ready to "get busy'.

Visitation Valley wasn't a match for Ducky and the boys.

Sean Hannon the red headed pitcher and Mike Bishop the catcher, switched spots after the first game. Bishop was the leading hitter, going four for four. He had a double and a triple to go along with two singles. He also had two hits in the first game with three RBI's.

"Nice game boys" Ducky told the team "12 to 2. We hit really good and played great on defense. Red Rat you pitched great, Bish! Nice job behind the dish, Little Joe made some great catches. Johnny? How's your lip? Use your glove next time!"

Johnny took a wicked hop in the third inning off his mouth. It took an inning to stop the bleeding. It puffed up pretty good after a while.

"Been hit harder than that" Johnny Smiled.

"Might be tough Kissing you know who!" Little Joe popped off and began laughing

As expected, everyone else started laughing. Johnny threw the baseball he was holding at Joe and missed. Joe started running down Jerrold towards Newhall giggling with Johnny on his heels. Just behind the both of them was Danny laughing and Kenny Miles bringing up the rear yelling

"Wait for me Boys"

Chapter Two

Not much was happening these days in the "Old Barbary Coast" area of San Francisco. Once known as the wickedest place on earth, it was reduced to just a few dance halls on Pacific Ave. The Bella Union and the Hippodrome still remained as the last two of the twenty-four-hour dance halls. At its busiest, before the 1906 earthquake and fire, the Barbary Coast extended five city blocks from Montgomery Street all the way to Stockton along Pacific Ave. and Broadway Ave... Chinatown, which bordered Pacific, added to the size of the area of about two miles. Not much of this area was flat. It was full of small hills, dead ends, dangerous narrow walking corridors without lighting and a network of underground catacombs. Within these two square miles, twenty-four hours of absolute mayhem took place seven days a week. Alcohol consumption was higher in that part of town than anywhere else on earth. Dance halls, like the Bella Union and the hundreds of small wooden "cribs", offered more prostitutes than any town in the world. Opium dens filled Chinatown. For over fifty years, this part of San Francisco catered to men from all parts of the world. The 1849 Gold Rush brought men not only to the gold fields of Northern California, but it also brought women and "entertainment" to the once small town located next to the greatest bay on the west coast.

The fire that followed the earthquake, burned down almost the whole area. The old wooden buildings went up in flames along with the area's businesses and reputation. Owners tried to rebuild and bring back what was once the busiest part of "the City", but they struggled. In 1914, San Francisco passed "The Red Light Abatement Act" making prostitution illegal. The World War in Europe took away thousands of men and the start of Prohibition came in 1919. These three events brought an end to the Barbary Coast and made room for a new beginning.

Most of the wealthy Italian families have moved out of what is now known as North Beach. Their mansions were dynamited and used as fire blocks for the fire after the earthquake. This area was originally named North Beach because of the nearby beach along the waterfront. Some of the residents of the city also called it "Little Italy" because of all of the Italians that lived there. As in most large cities, Prohibition launched organized crime. In San Francisco it was named the Cosa Nostra and "The Black Hand"! And it was present in North Beach.

Standing in front of The Hotel D'Oloran on Columbus Ave. was Luigi Malvese. Luigi worked for Genaro Broccolo who lived in the eight-story hotel. Luigi Malvese served Genaro as his driver, body guard and enforcer. Luigi's five foot seven 185-pound frame included a barrel chest, thick arms and short legs that were always covered with an expensive double breasted suit. Under a tilted wide brimmed hat, sat a mean face that had a pudgy nose, high cheek bones, thick black eye brows and tiny ears. At twenty-four, Luigi had risen through Genaro's "La Familia". He was actually the son of Genaro's sister, Rosa Malvese. His father Dominic was killed ten years earlier in a gun fight along Broadway Ave. helping protect Broccoli's interest at a house of prostitution.

Genaro Broccolo was the local "Godfather". He had risen to power through bootlegging and protection. He also controlled what little prostitution there was. Genaro had organized his local friends into a strong outfit during the rebuilding of "The City" after the fire. They were a ruthless bunch of thugs, who had no problems beating and killing women, children and the elderly. They were always looking for the next opportunity to build a bigger business. The fishing business on the nearby wharf was the real money maker though and he knew that! He needed to find his way into the wharf and organize the labor. He had several rivals in order to take control of the wharf. Nunzio Alioto was starting a small restaurant that sold lunchtime meals to the local Italian laborers. His "stall #8 was surrounded by a large lumber yard, train tracks, a union hall and many wholesale fisheries. Because his family also had fished there for many years, he was well respected by the locals. The other rival for control of the wharf was Frank Lanza. He too was a bootlegger and a loan shark. He was also beginning to get involved in the selling of drugs. Frank had begun his gang in a different part of the city called the Mission District. His group of hooligans did not get along with Genaro's and often had" differences with them in the drinking establishments. These three men and their families would battle it out over the next eight years to take control of the wharf. It would all start with friendly meetings on Wednesday mornings at Nunzio's stall #8.

On this Wednesday morning Genaro would be driven to the wharf by Luigi. Malvese knew the route that he was going to take but all he could think of right now, as he waited for the Godfather was the smell! The wind was blowing pretty good from the south and that brought with it "Butchertown"!

"Dam! How da hell do those freak en cowboys live with that shit smell?" Mr Brocollo said to Luigi as he climbed into the back seat of his black Ford four door sedan.

"Pretty bad ha Boss! I sure wouldn't want to live in that freak en hole" added Luigi as he closed the door.

On his way to the wharf and Nunzio's place, Malvese would stop at the Rosaia Florist Shop on the corner of Bay and Columbus. The Godfather loved his roses and he always wore one in his lapel. He thought it made him look special. Genaro was also a short round man of forty-two. He loved his pasta and red homemade vino. Now that he had people to do his dirty work, his body was not as hard as it used to be. Under his dark stripped suit, he wore a starched white long-sleeved shirt and suspenders to hold up his pants. He didn't like using a belt because it would not hide his ever-growing belly! His hat covered a balding head that included a pencil thin mustache, a furrowed brow and dark almost black piercing eyes.

As Luigi walked through the front door of the florist shop, he waved to Enrico and Pietro Rosaia, who were cutting flowers at one of the counters. They were two of three Rosaia brothers that owned and worked the florist shop which they opened after the fire had burned down their vegetable store in 1906. The brothers had immigrated like many Italians before the turn of the century to live a better life. They left behind their parents, one brother and one sister in the small town of Verpiano, just above Florence, in the hills of Italy.

Life had not been easy for the three brothers, but things were starting to work out for them. Pietro had had the most troubles of the brothers. He and his wife Kate, lost their first born, a daughter, at birth. After having a son and three baby girls, Kate died from complications after a short battle with lobar pneumonia in 1921. It was difficult for Pietro to raise three little girls, a son and work long hours. So, after two months, each brother took on a daughter to live with them. Adele, the youngest, went to Enrico and his wife Celia who lived at 1415 Kearney Street in a three-story flat. Just above the old Barbary Coast.

Kate and Pietro were a great looking couple and very happy together. Pietro stood six feet two inches. Which was very tall for that time. He had blond hair, as all of his brothers had. He just had more of it! His wide shoulders and long legs gave him a very athletic looking body. Blue eyes set off the appealing face that most people thought of as friendly looking.

Kate was of dark skin and average height. On the small side, she had beautiful dark brown eyes that fit the perfect nose. Her long black hair sat with cascading waves to her shoulders. She had a tiny waist that made her shoulders look wide. She was by far the most attractive woman in the area.

They had met at the local church dance and instantly felt the connection that stayed with them until her passing. In fact, Pietro would never again find that same feeling and had no desire to remarry..

"Coma stain Luigi! What are we going with today? A beautiful dark red or this bright white rose?"

Pietro was always outgoing to Luigi. Even though he disliked the man. Luigi could make things difficult on the brothers if he wanted. As Pietro walked towards the cooler of the long stem roses, Enrico went to the register to grab the weekly envelop that was owed to The Godfather for protection from the Lanza gang!

"Pietro, I'm not sure. So, I'll take one of each. Understand! All of the conversation was in Italian, including the hand gestures. It made for a colorful exchange!

Smiling, Pietro reached for a red and white long stem rose. It was about one year ago that the brothers didn't come up with the envelop for two weeks. Luigi Malvese and his "little" brother Guido, paid a visit to the oldest brother, Amadeo Rosaia, during lunch one day. Guido drug Amadeo outside to the street and broke his arm and nose, while Luigi made sure everyone watched. Luigi needed to send a message to all of his "customers" that they needed to pay and pay on time!

"Thanks boys" As Luigi grabbed the envelop from Enrico and took a smell of the roses that Pietro handed him.

"Next Wednesday I'll be back." He said in a laughing tone.

"Oh, my brother Guido passes his best on to Amadeo. He hopes his nose and arm are much better these days." as he danced out the front door.

Luigi opened the backdoor of the beautifully waxed black car that had spoken wheels and white wall tires. Luigi gave Genaro the white rose. *"This will look great Sir, with your white Fedora"*

Enrico watched through the window as Luigi placed the red rose in his lapel before he got in the driver's seat of the eight windowed Ford.

"Tessa Malinda. (Shit head) Someday Pietro, we've got to figure out a way to not have to pay that man."

"Agreed Enrico. There has got to be a way out of this situation. I believe what they are doing is illegal. But how do we approach the Police? Suppose they are in with Genaro?"

Pietro was the biggest of the three brothers. Although he had a friendly face, he also had the worst temper of the brothers, but he was good at not showing it. Although he wasn't as big as Guido Malvese, he was close. He felt when the time was right, the brothers would even things up for what Guido had done to Amadeo. He didn't like making those payments and he sure didn't enjoy Luigi taking the free roses!

"Enrico, tonight I need to come to your home and visit with my little angle Gina."

Pietro and his son Edward (fourteen years old) lived with Kate's parents. He really loved his daughters and missed them all, but he just could not take care of all of them the way he should. Gina the youngest, lived the closest and was the easiest to visit.

"How's my little girls English coming along?"
When she moved in with Enrico and Celia, Gina spoke only Italian. It was important to Celia that Adele only spoke English and it upset her when she didn't! After two years of living on Kearny Street and speaking only English and attending Garfield Elementary School, she was doing great.

"Ah Pietro! Tut to bene, until she gets mad!"

Enrico said with a big smile. He loved it when Gina spoke Italian, because then he would too! Which really upset his wife!

Gina already had an interesting life for a seven-year-old. Besides living with her aunt and Uncle and their family, she had also survived a mini epidemic of the serious disease, diphtheria, which had hit the North Beach area. One of her playmates, Adele Mortimer, died from the bacterial infection. Its final damage came from her kidneys shutting down and complications from her heart. Gina's symptoms reached a point where her airway was getting blocked by material causing difficulty in breathing. The Doctors were able to help Gina get back to being a healthy little girl because they finally figured out what they were fighting. With Adele, it all happened too fast. Gina's other close friend and cousin, Marion, who lived on the first floor of the flat on Kearny Street with her parents Selinda and Henry Arata, fortunately didn't have any complications. Gina and Marion cried for days after the loss of their best friend. To help Adele deal with her friend's death, Enrico bought her a little black and white puppy. Teddy was a long-haired mutt that would follow Gina everywhere she went. Teddy also slept on the kitchen floor at night next to Gina's bed.

Gina was also a smart little girl in school. She spent one week as a second-grade student before they passed her to the third grade. After one month, Gina was moved again, this time into the fourth grade. Reading had become a passion because it allowed her to learn about new places and introduced her to many make-believe people. Celia spent a lot of time teaching Gina many new cards games. These games helped Gina think quickly and also helped her with her other favorite subject, Arithmetic. One of Celia's other favorite things to do with her little niece was to attend the movie shows on Pacific Ave. Of course, Teddy would tag along with them and always be waiting outside for them when the show was over!

Pietro's monthly visits to Kearny Street, which also included dinner with everyone, started after Gina's recovery from diphtheria. All three floors of the flat were occupied by Celia's side of the family. Sister Selinda, husband Henry and Gina's best friend Marion, lived on the first floor. Emilia, Celia's other sister, lived on the second floor with husband Archie Trampoline and their children; Ernie, Raymond and Edna. Living on the top floor of the flat was the Rosaia family, which included son Alfred and little Gina. The other child Agnes, had just married Charlie Lagomarsino, also a florist, and they lived close by on Greenwich. The flat on Kearny was originally built by the sister's father before the earthquake and fire and had to be rebuilt after, just like the rest of the neighborhood. The Flat was halfway up Kearny Ave. It was a very steep hill that would challenge the best drivers and their ability to use a clutch. The top of Kearny was a dead end. It was at the base of Nob Hill which would eventually be the location of Coit Tower. The North Beach area was much like many areas of San Francisco at the time. Many hills and streets that would wind down them. Getting up the cobbled stone streets were difficult, going down could be dangerous.

Celia was born and raised in San Francisco. Her father was one of the early Italians who emigrated to the new city after the gold rush of 1849. Her father started out as a fisherman, like many of the young Italians, but he changed his thinking and became a florist. There seemed to be a lot of fisherman and not many flower shops! Business was good. Many new businesses were starting up and because of the gold rush people had money to spend on non-essentials. Celia took in little Gina and treated her well. But not as though she was her daughter. It took her time to eventually fall in love with Gina as her daughter. Enrico was just the opposite. He always thought of Gina as his daughter and always introduced her to people as his daughter. Life was not easy for Gina.

"Papa, Papa" Gina yelled out as she ran to the door. She greeted her father first with a great big hug and of course the seven-year-old also received the usual hug from Uncle Henry as she called him!

"How's my little angle?" Pietro loved to call Gina that. She looked so much like his wife Kate and always reminded him of all the great times they had together. They really had a deep love for each other.

"What did you learn today in school?" Pietro knew that school was important to his daughter and it was something she liked to tell him about.

"It was wonderful Papa. My teacher, Miss Frizz, let me read a story out load to the class. We also spent time in the library looking for a book to read."

"That's great! Let's sit for dinner and you can tell me all about the book" After a long day's work, the two brothers were hungry and several glasses of Enrico's homemade wine would accompany

dinner. Alfred joined the family as they ate Celia's famous tortellini, minestrone soup and sourdough bread from the wharf. Everyone laughed and had a good time. Gina would always slip Teddy a few scrapes from the dinner table.

After dinner, father, daughter and Teddy went for their walk down Kearny to Broadway, over to Grant and back up the small hill and cross back over on Union Street to Kearny. They talked about many things, but always they talked about Kate. Pietro wanted Gina to know what a wonderful mother and wife she was. Gina continually wanted to hear a new story about her mother. Gina would think about how some day she too would be a great mother and wife. This story telling and time with his youngest daughter was also great for Pietro. It also made him very sad to leave. He would have to wait another month or so before he would return.

Four o'clock came early for Gina and Teddy. Each morning at this time, Gina was up and had the coffee going. With her bed put away in the small closet in the kitchen that also had held her clothes, it gave everyone more room for breakfast. Enrico would be joined by his son Alfred. The twenty-five-year-old worked as a flower buyer for the family florist shop. He also bought the flowers for Charlie and Agnes, who's florist shop was on Geary Blvd.

Gina would make sure that along with the coffee, the men would have fresh fruit, an egg and the local bread with olive oil. Gina didn't drink coffee, but she loved the fresh fruit and bread. So did Teddy!

After the morning meal was eaten by the two men, Gina cleaned things up and got herself ready for school. Celia would prepare her own breakfast. Usually, Gina and Teddy would go downstairs and play with Marion until it was time to walk to school. Garfield Elementary was just up the street one block on Filbert.

The area was busy with a lot of rebuilding. The streets were steep and covered in cobble stones. The stones made different sounds depending on what was pounding on them. On top of the hill overlooking the bay was a park that was donated to the city of San Francisco. On this property, one of the rich Italian families who had moved to a different part of town, was building a big structure. The widow who was donating this building and the property surrounding it wanted to call it Coit Tower.

Chapter Three

"*Morning Mr Allen. It's a wet one today!*" Young John Turnbull had all of his Call-Bulletin newspapers covered so that they would not get wet from the cold November rain. He made good use of Cyril DeNike's Restaurant and its entry way on the corner of Third and Galvez. Johnny had been working this corner for two years now and at thirteen years old enjoyed the extra work plus he loved working for a newspaper. He was like his own boss! He would walk up and down Third Street selling his morning newspapers for five cents to the hard-working men of Butchertown... Johnny also made sure he was at the corner of Evens Ave. when the 29-car dropped off more workers. He had worked hard at tripling the amount of papers sold that the previous boy had done. Johnny might be late for school a lot, but the money was too good.

"*Johnny you're a hard-working young man! After the start of the new year, how'd you like to come work for me?*"

Being asked by Mr. Allen himself was a big deal. What a great opportunity Johnny thought. He'd have to quit going to school though. Asking "Ma" would be difficult, but a chance to work at Allens was too good of an opportunity to miss. Allens was one of the four biggest slaughter houses in Butchertown and getting bigger all of the time. And you don't say "*No*" to Mr. Allen.

"*Sounds great Mr. Allen. But ... I have one condition*"

"*Johnny, you sure as hell got some balls. That's one of the reasons why I like you!*" Mr. Allen had a big smile on his face. Either this kid was not very smart or he had something special about him. He also had known Johnny's father in the past and was one of the few business men in the area who respected him. Rock Turnbull was a lot of things, but he was a man of his word.

"*What's your condition?*"

"*You got room for my friend Little Joe? He needs work too! Little Joe and I have always talked about working for you and I can't take that job without him coming along too. It wouldn't be right*"

Mr. Allen looked at the wet young kid "*Loyal too! I know you two have been working for your uncle's place for a few years*" as he paused and thought for a second or two. "*I will need an extra person on clean up with ole Marv Bernhagen. You two come see me after the New Year and I'll get you started. You know Leo Federico? You'll work with his crew*"

"*THANK YOU, Mr. Allen. THANK YOU! We'll work our ass er tails off for you!*"

Johnny was so excited he could barely keep from yelling out loud and watched Mr. Allen turn the corner on Evan's Ave. Johnny still had an hour of selling papers in the rain before he and Little Joe would walk the muddy streets with Danny and Ken on their way to school.

"Your shit' en me Johnny, really?" Little Joe stopped walking and looked in his best friend's eyes to see if he was *"pulling his leg".* *"No way. There is No way, you're kidding me!"*

"Nope" Johnny replied *"Mr. Allen wants us to come see him after the New Year. It will take us that long to convince your parents to let you quit school and work full time."* He laughed

"Well, what about your Ma? You know how she feels about school and all"

"Joe my friend, I can get her to think my way. It's you I'm worried about"

"Ha! Your Ma ain't Nellie! As he began to run towards Ken Miles house giggling.

School took forever to get over for both of the boys. School usually did anyway, but this day just seemed to go extra slow. Neither of the boys could really remember what went on that day in the classroom. Work at Turnbull's went a lot faster. The boys were a lot bigger and stronger; they could get more done and they seemed to have more freedom. Johnny's uncles didn't ride them as much and let them work. As they worked, both of them kept thinking about how they would tell their families about the great opportunity at Allen's.Little Joe was really grateful to Johnny for many things. It was something else to have a great friend. The two of them had so many adventures together already and would have more to come in the future.

Usually, the walk to Turnbulls Slaughter House from school was uneventful. The four boys always walked a different route down to Evens Ave. Today they decided to run over to the stock pens on Innes Street and check out the animals. Guess who was there? Gilberto and his buddies.

"Hey Chico!" Gilberto who hadn't seen Johnny for a while said with a smirk.

"Long time no see Bert"

"It's Gilberto!"

Johnny found a burnt piece of wood on the ground with a little mud on it. Picked it up and tossed it to the now 15-year-old from the Potrero Hill

"Put up or shut up"

Johnny now stood face to face with his old advisery!

The remaining six boys sized each other up knowing full well what was going to happen next. Gilberto placed the block on his left shoulder.

The strange feeling a guy gets before he fights hit Johnny. It quickly turned to anger and then to rage.

Thinking that Gilberto would be ready for the same one two, he faked the swipe with his right hand to get Gilberto to move his left hand to block. Johnny sent a straight left to the face and followed with his right to Gilberto's jaw. This time there was no smile from Gilberto. He fell backwards. And Turnbull was on him.

At the same time Little Joe, Danny and Ken joined the fun and got after the three other Potrero boys.

With his left arm over hooking the surprised Gilberto's right arm, Turnbull turned his left hip into him and forced his shoulder down causing Gilberto to put his left hand on the ground to catch his balance. That gave the now same sized Irish boy a free right hand. And he used it. Four, five times to the different parts of the face. Gilbert went limp from the blows. Johnny flung his left arm free as his opponent fell to the dirt. With his right footed boot, Johnny swung tree times to Gilbert's face directed to his mouth. A few teeth fell to the ground. Gilbert's face was a mess as Johnny stood over him with his fist clinched. His only movement was his chest breathing. Turnbull got down to Gilbert's face and yelled

"Nice try Bert"

Johnny got to his feet and looked around and watched the carnage of the results of the other three separate fights going on. The Boys from Butchertown walked away arms over arms laughing on their happy way along the dirt road.

As always, Ma had dinner ready for Johnny when he got home from Turnbulls Slaughter House. He had so much to be grateful for too. Ma was an amazing woman. She had taken care of both Rita and John as if they were her own children. His Aunt Lizzy was only to keep Johnny for a little while, but she just could not give him up! She loved both of the children so much, and wanted them to be something special because she believed they were. They enjoyed many hearts to heart talks over dinners. They didn't keep secrets. Telling Me that he wanted to quit school was not something he was looking forward to. She put a great value in education. But he did talk her into letting him work the corner newspaper job in the mornings!

"Ma, I got some great news today"

"John, it's always nice to get good news. I hope I like it!" Aunt Lizzy was a smart lady. Having raised Johnny for the last twelve years, she knew something was up.

She and her husband had lived at the Galvez home before the turn of the century. Her husband John, tragically died at an early age while he was working at the Pacific Rolling Mill, just below Irish Hill. They had not been married long when the accident happened, and they had no children. Over the years she worked as a seamstress, but lately had relied on Johnny and Rita for the household income.

"Mr. Allen himself offered Little Joe and I a job. He wants us to come see him after New Years." Johnny didn't look up as he continued to eat his beef stew with mushy vegetables.

"Hum... You can't quit working at Turnbull's, you can't quit going to school, you have your newspaper job. When, may I ask, are you going to squeeze this new job in?" Aunt Lizzy then sat

at the table right across from Johnny and looked right at him. Not giving him a chance to answer her.

"Look at me son."

Johnny knew he was in for a serious talk now. Son was not used by Ma very often. Only when things got really important.

"Ma... This is too great of an opportunity for me to miss out on. I'm going to quit going to school and work all three jobs! We need the money! Plus, I know how to read and write and I'm good at arithmetic. That's all I need. Heck, I read the newspaper every day. I even know what's going on in the world. More so than most adults."

"I promised your father when I took you in, that I'd make sure you would be raised a good Catholic, that you'd be an honest hard worker and that you would get your schooling. He made sure that his brothers would take you on at work and that they would also provide us with a little extra each month. I can't go back on my promise!"

"Ma ... You've done good and you're not going back on any promise. I will be all of those things and more. I have the schooling to be what I want to be. I promise you Ma that you will be proud of me. I don't need school anyway. My father finished school. Didn't help him any. Look how he turned out. And that money that my family was to pay you, stopped when my father died. I need to start taken care of us, cause no one else cares about us. We are on our own!"

By this time in his life, thirteen years old, Johnny had found out many things about his mother and father. He could not change what had happened, but he would make sure that things would turn out differently for him. Through the last few years, he had conversations with quite a few people about his father. The most reliable were with Aunt Lizzy and Rita. These long talks lead him to finding out why his family didn't want him. It hurt him deeply and he would never forgive any of them! He had to work for them, only to help Lizzy, Rita and himself. His anger for them would last a lifetime. Ma loved him for who he was. He would NEVER let her down.

Johnny's father, Robert L. was the oldest child of seven. He was born in 1868 to Robert D. and Margaret in San Francisco. His parents had come to California from New York to get away from the Irish gangs and lifestyle there. As a butcher, his father quickly settled in the part of San Francisco that was newly designated for that type of work. Butchertown! And there was plenty of work.

As a young man growing up, he found himself not only learning the family business as a butcher, but taking care of his brothers and sisters as they made their way through school. He fought many battles for his younger siblings until he came out of high school. Living the type of lifestyle of his father did wasn't something he wanted to do. He wanted something a little more exciting.

After high school Robert began working at one of the four main slaughter houses in the area, H. Moffat Company. At the time, it was built on pilings over Islais Creek. His job was the knocker on the kill floor. He spent his days swinging a three-pound sledge hammer to the heads of all the animals to be slaughtered. Two things happened to him. "Rock" Turnbull as he later would be called, became a very well-built young man with great strength and endurance. He also became immune to the sound and feelings of crushing a living skull. Both would serve him well in his future.

Irish Hill, in 1890's San Francisco, became the poor man's Barbary Coast. Many of the single Irish immigrants lived in shacks,cottages and forty boarding houses on the hill, which was located about two miles from Railroad Street (which became Third Street), just west of Butchertown.

Also, on Irish Hill were "Hotels" for the entertainment for all of the young Irish lads. Some of the "Hotels" were called; The Green House, The White House, The San Quentin,The Cash Hotel, and the Monterey House. Dancing girls, prostitution,gambling, cheap beer and whiskey and a lot of fighting took place on a nightly basis.

Every Saturday afternoon in a hay rope ring outside of Jim Galely's Hotel (The San Quentin), the boys and men from each Hotel would challenge each other. After the fights, they would all go over to Boyles Steam Dump and drink steam beer for a nickel a beer. It took Robert one Saturday afternoon of seeing the action at Galely's and Boyles to know that this was what he wanted to experience. In order to get between the hay ropes though, he needed to work for one of the Hotels. After several weeks of asking around he found work at The Monterey House as a "grunt". He worked nights cleaning bathrooms, glasses, changing kegs and anything else the bartenders didn't want to do. He continued working days at Moffats as a knocker until The Monterey House could work into something more than being a "grunt". Evan though he still lived with his family on Oakdale, Robert began to spend the nights at The Monterey House. His parents did not like what was happening to their oldest son!

He also had great success between the hay ropes at Galey's. The boys from The San Quentin were parolees that worked in the mills at the foot of the Hill. They always made for a good fight. The "Rocks" first few fights came against those San Quentin boys, but they didn't last long because of his overpowering strength. Each Saturday brought him a new and better opponent. But he kept winning. Jimmy Cole, who owned The Monterey House, took notice. He changed The Rocks job to bartender, which paid more money but also brought him more responsibilities. He had to learn how to watch over the dancing girls, which meant collecting money for their services. He was a natural at breaking up fights! Armed with a shillelagh stick and his growing reputation, things never got out of control. He knew how to crack heads! Not only had Rock risen to the number one bartender, but in the four years that he had been fighting, he became the so-called champion of the hay ropes. His strength and stamina were matched by a strong chin and a will to win. That's where the name "The Rock" came from. He was like hitting a rock!

The Rock was living an exciting life and had stopped working at Moffatts. In the four years that he had worked at The Monterey, he was making more money than he did while working on the kill floor and it was a whole lot more fun and exciting. Jimmy Cole liked him so much that at the age of twenty-four he pretty much ran the place. His parents and family members didn't like the fact that he was working at a "Hotel". Also, most of a quintessence's now, were members of the Irish gangs and dance hall girls. He had his own room there and all of his meals were taken care of. With each week, each month and each year, Robert was becoming distant from his family. They had gone two different ways. Rock Turnbull had built himself quite a reputation on Irish Hill and in Butchertown. Everyone knew who he was and what he did. It had a big effect on his family. People looked at them as not good people, because of his nasty reputation of a skull crusher, mean disposition and affiliation with the Irish gangs.

Deep down inside Robert didn't like what he had become and wanted out of his lifestyle. Making a change would be difficult but he would eventually find a way.

After the turn of the century in 1902, William Turnbull Roberts closest brother in age, married a Butchertown girl from Quesada Ave. named Mary Loughran. Rock Turnbull came to the wedding as the best man. At that time the tradition was that the oldest brother would stand up as the best man. William was hoping Rock wouldn't make the wedding, so that Edward would instead be his best man. The relationship between the two oldest brothers was not a very good one! Plus, William didn't want anything bad to happen at the wedding because trouble usually followed Rock. At the wedding, Robert was a perfect gentleman. He avoided trouble, because he too didn't want any. Mary Loughran's younger sister Lillian, was her maid of honor. Lillian was so much different than the painted ladies that Robert had become accustomed to being around. She was not an attractive woman. Some woman can really stick out in a room because of the way they dress and carry themselves. Lillian was a quiet, slight twenty-two-year-old. Robert spent a lot of the evening with Lillian. He did notice how pretty she was. That night was the first night that he could remember, of not having to be Rock Turnbull. He really enjoyed himself and being around Lillian. Others remarked how different he was that night.

Lillian was somewhat leery of Robert at first. She had heard so many stories about him. None of them being good! He was well dressed and good looking, but what attracted her to him was how soft spoken he was. He also never talked about himself or his present-day work. She did most of the talking, which was very unusual for her. Robert was very easy to be around and she had always been uneasy around older men. Lillian really enjoyed the evening, but thought that she would most likely never see Robert again.

Over the next four years things didn't change much. The Rock no longer fought between the hay ropes. He did that long enough to earn his reputation. The seven nights a week at The Monterey House was taking its toll on him. Work was no longer fun and exciting and it was becoming difficult!

On April 18th 1906 at 5:12 am local time, life changed for everyone living in San Francisco. The fires that followed the famous earthquake burned over 80 % of the city. Irish Hill and its old wooden shakes, boarding homes and Hotels quickly turned to ashes. The slaughter houses over Islais Creek had crumbled into the creek from the massive shaking. Much of Butchertown was not affected by the fires. With dirt streets and plenty of room between homes, fires didn't travel easily. Irish Hill and Dog Patch, another small neighborhood of immigrant mill workers, lost everything. With over 3,500 workers in Butchertown and the need for wholesale meats, Butchertown was rebuilt in a hurry. This time not over the Creek but just a few blocks away!

Robert looked at this as an opportunity to start over. He had saved some money, in fact he had enough he thought to start his own business. But not on Irish Hill. He talked his brothers into joining him and starting Turners Slaughter House. He used his saved money to buy the property and building on Evans Ave about four blocks from Third Street and the railroad. They began their small operation in 1907. Over the next two years, Robert put all of his efforts into building a strong business. He used his experience at the Hotel and also his connections in the area. He drove himself and his brothers very hard. They all worked long hours, but with twenty or more new slaughter houses in the area they had too. Business was good but also very competitive. Rock's reputation both helped the business and hurt it. Because some of his connections were with "shady" people, there were those who would not do business with him and his brothers. Those who did, found out that his word was very good and slowly people were looking at him differently.

Free time among the Turnbull brothers wasn't much. What little time Robert had, he spent visiting with Lillian Loughran or as he began to call her Lilly. The two were a perfect match for each other. Lillian really didn't get along with her family either. So, the two of them enjoyed their time together without family members around. They loved to go to the silent movies along with the vaudeville acts at the South San Francisco Opera House. Sundays when the weather was good, they would take the trolley to Chutes at the Beach. They would enjoy the amusement park and its famous ride "Shoot the Chutes". Trout Baths, a six-pool seawater complex was also a place of fun along with a quite dinner at The Cliff House.

After two years of courtship, they married and settled in a little house in Butchertown. The house on Lane Street was just around the corner from his parents' home on Oakdale and easy walking distance over the dirt streets to Evans Ave and work. At forty-two years old, Robert finally felt good about himself again. He had a wonderful wife, a respectable job and a family on the way. Lilly lost their first child at birth, a little girl, but they continued on and had Margaret in 1913. Son Robert followed along in 1915. After Roberts birth Lilly began to have problems. She became delusional and had attacks of depression. She would think that people were conspiring against her. Ten months after giving birth to her son, she was admitted to the California State Hospital for the insane in Sacramento. Her younger sister and grandmother were living at the same kind of hospital in Napa. Robert made many trips to visit Lilly hoping things would change and she would get better. Three days after Christmas in 1916, Lillian Loughran passed away. Little Robert had already began living with Aunt Lizzy on Galvez and Margaret started off living with William and his family. Rock continued to work at the slaughter house driving himself and his brothers even harder. He was paying Lizzy O'Brien money to take care of Robert. He would visit his son on Sundays and on Sunday nights he would spend time with daughter Margaret. As young as they were, they really never remembered his visits or him. His life of hard work on The Hill, fighting, drinking and being a heavy smoker combined with the depression of losing his family, life came to an end for him in April of 1918 at the age of 49.

Evan though they were brothers and worked together, there were some deep feelings of resentment. None of the family, including grandparents wanted anything to do with The Rocks son, and the son of an insane woman. They could only imagine how the boy would turn out. As the years went on, they treated Johnny terribly and convinced his sister that he would always be trouble and amount to no good.

Johnny, Rita and Aunt Lizzy talked about many things in the next month. This would be a "family" decision because it would affect all of them. Lizzy would make sure that Johnny's reasons for no longer attending school were well thought out. They would look at all of the positive and negative outcomes. Much to John's dismay, Aunt Lizzy spent time talking with Mr. Allen after mass on one of the Sundays.

Johnny knew he was a lot like his father in many ways. And that was not a bad thing! He knew that he liked excitement. After all, he never passed up a chance to "Knock someone's block off". He really liked the hard work of the slaughter house. What he wanted most of all, was to be the type of father that he never had. It would all start for him by saving his money, little by little so that he would be able to provide for a wife and kids. And so, it was decided that Johnny would start work for James Allens, but his work at Turnbull's would be cut in half. John had no problem with the compromise that Ma came up with. He felt that he could put some time in at Turnbull's, but the less time that he had to spend around the Turnbull's the better. Business had not been very good anyway. They would be losing their best butcher along with his friend, Little Joe as he too would only work at James Allens.

Chapter Four

To get to Saint Bridget's School for girls, Gina Rosaia had a long way to travel. After just turning ten in October of 1928, Gina was now in the eighth grade. The morning routine had not changed much for her other than she and Teddy had to walk four blocks down Kearney Street to Pacific Ave... There, she would get on a trolley for thirteen blocks to Franklin Street. The return would be the same route, as Teddy would always be waiting for her.

Saint Bridget's was a smaller Catholic school run and taught by the Nuns of the nearby Catholic Church. Although three years younger than the other girls of her grade, Gina was as tall or taller than most of the girls. She kept her black hair very short and parted slightly to the side. Of course, she wore no makeup, lip stick or ear rings. Her dresses were very simple because she made them herself. Her one expensive part of her wardrobe was her coat. It was a thick fur, lined inside to keep her warm on those cold foggy days that "The City" was famous for. Her grades in all of the subjects were also some of the highest. Gina made sure that she never missed school or was late. Sometimes she would spend time after school helping in the library with Sister Mary Ann, putting books away and any other jobs that needed to be done. Gina loved to learn and be at school. She often thought about what she wanted to do with her life.

"Sister Mary Ann! No one in my family has ever continued on to college after high school. I'm not really sure how someone goes to college. How does it work?"

"Well Gina, first you must have really good grades in high school. Then you would need to pass an entrance exam, and the most difficult part for you would be paying for it."

"Let's say that I did have the money to go to college. What do you learn about and how would it help me?

Gina knew that attending college would be difficult. Finding out about what went on there and what see could learn about became important to her.

"Oh, young lady! There is so much to learn about! It becomes your choice as to what you want to study. That's the fun part. You find out now in high school, what you like and what you are good at. You follow your interests. That's what leads you to your career of choice! By finishing with a college degree, you would be one of the few women out there with one."

Sister Mary Ann really enjoyed talking to all of the girls about what was out there for them. She was one of the few at that time that thought women were equal to men. And she saw great potential in Gina.

Gina didn't understand what a career was, but if it was something you got to choose, it had to be a good thing. She knew getting a good job was also important. At ten years old, Gina didn't know what a good job for a woman would be. Not too many women at that time held important positions

Somehow, this young confident girl would find out. What she really wanted though, was to be a part of her own family. She wanted to raise her children with her husband. Gina had those monthly talks with her father where she found out how much she missed not having her own parents all of the time. Uncle Henry and Celia were very nice to her, but she was not their daughter. And Gina knew it. Pietro treated her so much differently, and Gina could feel the difference. She often wondered how it would be to live with her real parents.

Life for a ten-year-old girl in North Beach was a lot different than a ten-year-old boy. The boys seemed like they were allowed to run free around the neighborhoods. Playing ball in the parks, fooling around near and on the wharf and even getting jobs, were all things that the boys could do on their own. Gina and Marion were not allowed out of the house without and adult, except to go to school. The two young girls spent most of their time together sowing clothes, ironing, knitting and doing other household chores. They learned how to make ravioli, tortellini, spaghetti sauce and other Italian meals. Celia loved to go to the movies, especially the new talkies. She would take the girls to the movie house on Pacific Ave. and then treat them to ice cream on their way home. They also played card games for entertainment and help Uncle Henry make his wine in the basement. Sundays were also another chance to get out of the house. Saint Francis of Assisi Church was a six-block walk. After mass was a social time for the adults as well as the children. They were allowed to play games and visit with each other while the adults sat and talked for several hours. Every once in a while, the women would play bingo games inside while the men played bounce ball outside and smoked their cigars.

The summer time was one of Gina's favorite times. She would get to spend a week at Amedeo Rosaia's farm with her two sisters, Eva who was five years older and Florence who was three years older. Eddie her brother, and the oldest sibling would drive Gina to the farm in Colma. Colma is about a ten-mile drive from the south part of San Francisco. This four or five day was the only time the Rosaia children got to be around each other. It wasn't fun and games though by any means. They spent the days doing outside chores; feeding the pigs and chickens, cleaning their pens, planting and harvesting the vegetables and the most important task of preparing all of the flowers for the flower shop on Mission Street. With Gina as an extra worker around the house, more things got done. Eva and Florence liked it when Gina showed up because of the extra help. When she left the two girls had to go back to doing all of the work. For Gina the physical work was not something she was used too but, the reward came in the evenings when the girls could become better acquainted. The three girls came in different sizes and shapes. The faces all looked the same as well as having thick black hair. Gina, was the tallest even though she was the youngest. Florence was the shortest and the heaviest of the three. She was not fat; it was just that the other two girls were so skinny! They really looked forward to the night that Eddie and their father Pietro came for dinner. They enjoyed each other so much. Gina always cried when she left. Always thinking how much she and her siblings missed out on being a family all of the time. Gina knew deep down in her heart that someday she would have that family that she missed out on.

Gina also had a strong friendship with her cousin Agnes. Agnes was Uncle Henry and Celia's daughter and oldest child. She was quite a few years older than Gina. Built like her mother, she was short, maybe five foot three, and very round. She wore her brown hair up in a bun and always dressed in fine clothes. When working at the store, Charlie liked her to ware make up and ear rings. Agnes had married Charlie Lagomarsino just before Gina had moved into the flat on Kearney

Street. Charlie's family were owners of one of the largest florist shops in Sacramento. Charlie was a smart business man with a whole lot of charm and charisma. He and Agnes opened up their first flower shop on Geary Blvd. in the mid 1920's. In the next several years Charlie became associated with Julius Eppstein and his wife. They thought a lot of Charlie, as he became like the son they never had. Julius was owner of the famous Saint Francis Hotel. Both he and his wife lived in the hotel and they gave Charlie and Agnes control of the new florist shop in the hotel as well as their old shop, now known as the Julius Eppstein Plaza Florist on Geary Blvd.

Agnes and Charlie were very good to little Gina. Agnes treated her like a little sister. The Saint Francis Hotel put on many events both social and political. Everything was extravagantly done and the florist shop provided all of the decorations as well as the flowers. Gina and Marion spent time helping with set ups and take downs of these events. While helping out, the two girls got to know Mrs. Eppstein. She immediately took a liking to the girls and often times invited them to some of the events. Not only would she invite them but she would buy them dresses so that they looked like they belonged. Being at large gatherings with rich adults was fun for the girls and in their new dresses they learned how to act like young ladies should. Charlie spent a lot of time with "Chickie". That's what he called Gina. He would teach her about the proper etiquette at these events because so she wouldn't become embarrassed by doing something wrong. And he also thought of Gina as someone special and enjoyed his time with her. She made him laugh and Charlie liked to have a good time. Charlie also knew everyone in town who was important on the society seen, and they all liked him. He had become an important man in San Francisco 's rich Social Society, and he like to show off little "Chickie". She was a big hit with the older Italian men because she would talk with them in Italian. Her smile, charming well-read personality and good looks also helped the conversations.

Agnes' brother Alfred, worked for Charlie also, buying flowers (usually from the Rosaia farm) delivering and helping set up arraigments for all of the events at the Hotel and other big events around town. He was also very nice to Gina, but being over twenty years older, he didn't pay much attention to the little girl.

Once a year Charlie and Agnes would take the family for a vacation in the small town of Santa Cruz. It was just south of Half Moon Bay along the coast about sixty miles south of San Francisco. It was a fun place for everyone to be. They would rent a large house in town that was close to the beach and the new amusement park. Uncle Henry loved the ten days away from work. He would bring along his homemade wine and play a lot of card games with Gina and Marion. They loved to walk along the beach in the mornings and at night, go to the dances. Charlie had taught "Chickie" and Marion all of the new and old dances. Sometimes Uncle Henry and Alfred would join in after they had several glasses of the homemade wine. Everyone always had a great time on these vacations and Gina was very thankful to Agnes and Charlie for all that they did for her and taught her.

Back in North Beach, the struggle for control of the area started to become contentious. Genaro Brocollo, along with Luigi Malvese and his soldiers, began to butt heads with Frank Lanza and his growing family.

The Rosaia brothers had moved their florist shop out of the area to Mission Street. Pietro, his son Eddie who was now 18 and bigger than his father, got together with Pietro's two brothers in law, John and Ernest Mortorella. The two brothers were in their mid-twenties and were known in the area as hot-tempered Italians who didn't like being told what to do. They made sure that when the Rosaia brothers moved their belongings out and to the new store, that they were around to make sure Luigi and his brother Guido Malvese didn't try to collect anything extra.

"Well, well well. If it ain't the two Mortorella Boys! What are you two hot heads here for?"

Luigi Malvese and his brother Guido had heard that the Rosaia brothers were moving their flower shop across town and they were there to collect the protection money.

"Ah, Luigi and Guido. Just who we thought would show up"

John, the oldest of the two Mortorella's had crossed paths with Luigi awhile back at the old Bella Union. They had argued over one of the dance hall girls. The bartenders got between the two of them before anything had happened.

"Ya see my brother Ernie and I are helping my brother-in-law Pietro and his family move their shop. And, just in case you two ass holes showed up to collect something that didn't belong to you, well ... we wanted to make sure if any more arms got busted, they'd be yours!"

Luigi was furious. *"You got no freak en business stick en your dago noses in this. You're going to get hurt!"*

As Luigi finished his sentence, Eddie and Pietro walked out from the back holding clubs. Amedeo and Enrico came thru the front door also holding clubs. Luigi and Guido were not ready for the encounter. They were counting on just two or three older frighted men. Not so this time! The six men were ready for something to happen. The years of having to give up their hard-earned money had come to an end. This was their time to stand up to Luigi!

Pietro stepped forward and said *"Not this time Luigi. You've taken too much over the years and you're not getting any more. So, Leave"*

"Pietro! Not a good move! You know we'll come and get you no matter where you go. And this time, this time it will be bad, really BAD. I'll bring more than Guido here. You're fucked boys."

"Not so fast Malvese." John walked right up in Luigi's face.

"Me and Frankie "The Hat" Lanza got a couple things in common. We both hate you and that fat bastard boss of yours Broccolo."

John and Ernie were not part of Frank Lana's gang, but they were friendly. They had done a few favors for them and knew that they had a few coming their way.

"And he's just looking for an excuse to get rid of you and him"

Which was true. Frank had been gaining strength as Genaro was losing his strong hold on the area.

"I don't think it would be a wise move to start something you ain't gone a win over a small amount of money". John said with a smile.

"All it will take is one call to Frankie"

Amedeo walked forward and pointed towards the front door *"Leave! Now!"*

Luigi and Guido pushed their way through the front door and got in the black sedan. And sped away. Guido had his hand in the air and gave the boys a one finger salute.

The friendly Wednesday meetings at Alioto's #8 stall on the wharf had stopped after Genaro "The Godfather" Brocollo and Nunzio Alioto found they could not see eye to eye on things. Frank Lanza didn't like either of the older Italians. He would continue to get a stronger hold on the drug and alcohol market, while Genaro was losing control of his protection racket. Nunzio was taking control of the fisherman and the work on the wharf. The union that they were apart of had weak leadership and it was only a matter of time before Nunzio would take full control. Over the next four years things would become very violent as the three Italians worked to gain a strong hold on the whole area.

Chapter Five

After spending three and a half years working on the "Kill "floor for James Allens and Sons doing different jobs for Leo Federico and is crew of 55 workers, Jack Allen had something new for eighteen-year-old John Turnbull

Jack approached Johnny on a Friday morning while the crew was setting up for the lamb kill. Leo, still chewing on a half-burnt cigar, was getting things organized with the corral, making sure the Judas sheep were ready to go. Everyone else was having the morning smoke.

"Johnny, got a second?"

Tossing his cigarette to the floor, Johnny answered *"Sure! What's up Mr. Allen?"*

"Jack! It's Jack! My Dad is Mr. Allen! Anyway, how'd you like to try something different?"

Johnny was always up for new things around Allen's. *"What ya got on your mind?"*

"I'd like you to start working with Big John on the trucks. Learning how the routes work. Loading and selling. Give you a small bump in pay."

Big John Bishop was one of a few drivers that Allens was now using. He had spent time serving as a Marine in the "Great War". Big John served eight years as a Marine with the last four in transportation. He was a master mechanic a great driver and leader of men. Perfect for his position at Allen's. And tough. No one gave Big John a hard time. Bald with greasy hands, a thin cigar in the side of his mouth and bulging biceps went along with 215 pounds. He would teach Johnny the ropes and how to drive. Johnny already had the chops as a salesman from his experience as a newspaper boy. Johnny also would be working with his old baseball teammate Mike Bishop, Big Johns brother.

"Sounds like a great idea Jack! When do I start?" Johnny was excited for the new opportunity.

"As soon as you can get down to the Teamsters Union Hall and get a card. Leave a little early today and grab the 29-car going down town. You got a driver's license right?"

"Dam! Not yet! We'll figure out a way to get one and we'll get you started"

For Johnny, there hadn't been a reason to have a license. He walked everywhere or took the trolleys. Rita owned a car and he'd driven it a few times. Learning how to use the clutch was kinda fun. He just needed to get her to take him to the DMV and take the test.

Johnny no longer worked at Turnbull's Slaughter House. H. Moffatt Company, one of the four last slaughter houses, bought out Turnbulls just after the stock market crash in 1929. The Turnbull family got a good price and jobs with Moffatt's, which was right across the street from Allens on Evans Ave. Moffatts was using Turnbulls as a place for cooking and packaging sausage and processing pork bellies into bacon.

Johnny and Joe Dalpagetto, best friends forever, had been working as butchers together for ten years, Johnny for twelve! The two longtime friends still palled around with Ken Miles and younger Danny Carey. The difference was those two were in school all day while Johnny and Little Joe worked. Ken and most of the kids in the area attended Commerce High School out in Visitation Valley. Danny went to Galileo High School on Van Ness and Bay near North Beach. His parents felt he would get a better education there. The Butchertown four still loved to hang out at the corral on the weekends. Johnny was learning how to bulldog cows, while Joe wanted to rope steers. Danny was going to do the same as Johnny. Why not? Who needed fingers when he still had thumbs to bulldog. Ken just wanted to watch and give some encouragement!

It was also a great chance for Johnny to watch Nellie race and rope. They still enjoyed talking on those Saturday afternoons without anyone really noticing. If there was a good movie playing, they would meet at Mooney's on Third and LaSalle for a milkshake and walk together the five blocks to Palou Ave and the theater. Afterwards, Johnny would walk Nellie home, which was passed his sister Margret's house on Oakdale and around the corner on Newcomb. You could say that they were each others "steady" but neither would admit it. Johnny had no interests in any other girls and Nellie didn't have time for any other boys.

Nellie Bloom at seventeen, was still attending All Hallows School and she and her friend Marion Turnbull were getting ready for their senior year. Marion had been "Duck" Ma honey's girl for quite a few years now. Duck had played baseball for the University of San Francisco for two seasons before signing on to play for the Oakland Oaks professional team. Johnny and Nellie, Duck and Marion often went to dances together at the Native Son's of California's hall which was located on Revere Street.

During that summer of 1933, those four would talk about school. John kinda missed it. Duck encouraged Johnny to return for his senior year. Joe Dalpagetto had also begun to talk to Johnny about going back, but not for schools' sake and learning.

"Johnny. You know if we went back to school, we could play football!"

Both of them had fallen in love with the game. They had spent some of those Saturday afternoons watching college football at Kezar Stadium in Golden Gate Park. Santa Clara University and Saint Mary's College had built programs that were rivaling Note Dame. Along with The University of California, the three played in front of huge crowds. It was exciting. It was also a sport that fit both of their physical abilities and they loved to watch it. They had played some pickup games at the corral with the older cowboys and loved it. The game of football would become a lifetime of entertainment for the both of them. In the future, they would spend Sundays watching Professional football at the same Kezar Stadium together.

"Geez Joe. We'd have to stop working. I don't know?"

Johnny really liked the idea, but this was a time that people were looking for work. The Great Depression which started in 1929 wasn't quite over yet.

"I know. Let's talk with Jack Allen about it. He can tell us if it's a good idea"

Jack Allen was disappointed to hear that the two wanted to go back to school. They worked hard and they did a great job for him and his father.

"There are no guarantees that we'll have work for you two. But I can always give you a good recommendation if you try to get on somewhere else."

Butchertown was down to the four main slaughter houses. At its peak, Butchertown employed over 3,500 workers. With the depression, the demand for the different types of meat wasn't as high as before the stock market crash of 1929. With the low demand, there were less workers. And those that did work became specialized and unionized.

"Shit Joe, I'm in. It'll only be until November or December and we'll be back to work. Three maybe four months. I've saved enough to get Ma and I through those months."

It was just a few months of his life, and it would be his chance to play football.

Ma had mixed emotions. She knew Johnny really wanted to do this and after all, she could never say no to him! He had been a loyal hard worker his whole life. He had taken care of her as though she was his real mother. He needed to have some time off from work anyway. After this adventure, he was going to work for the rest of his life.

Little Joe and Johnny registered for their senior years at two different schools. Ma wanted Johnny to attend Galileo High School which was downtown off Van Ness and Bay Streets. Little Joe ended up at Commerce High School, near Visitation Valley.

At least Johnny would be able to go to school with Danny Carey. Ken Miles and Joe would run around together with each other at Commerce. Little Joe knew more guys there because they used to play baseball against them and most of the Butchertown kids went to school there also.

Galileo High School had won the City Championship in football in 1932 and would again contend for the title in '33. Although Johnny knew the rules of the game and how to play, learning how to play organized football was difficult. All of the other boys had played for two and three seasons and knew the system of plays and what the coach wanted.

Coach Ras Johnson decided that Johnny would have his best chance learning how to play end in the single wing offense and end on their six two defenses. It was like learning a new language! Words like; counter, cadence, trap, power, buck option, buck sweep, hole, blocking back and alignments seemed overwhelming. Learning basic movements, like a three-point stance and how to block out of it without standing straight up along with how to tackle properly without getting run over were not easy. Those first two weeks of practice were brutal. As tough as he thought he was, he got beat up pretty good. The others were playing at a faster speed than he could because they weren't thinking as much as Johnny was.

He liked being part of the team though. The other players were helping him learn about the game and getting him better. He loved the physical part of the game and slowly he began to improve. After three games which Galileo won, Johnny finally learned his plays! Now that he knew what he was doing, he began to improve at a faster rate.

Mean time over at Commerce High, Little Joe was having great success. He was the fastest player on the team, and they used his speed by giving him the ball to run. Joe was a natural runner and, in their offense, Joe didn't have to block. He either got the ball or they faked it to him. On defense, he played "safety". His job was to keep everyone in front of him, stay as deep as the deepest. He would only have to tackle anyone if they broke through the line. Teams very seldom passed the ball, but that was like playing centerfield in baseball!

Football was somewhat like baseball when it came to substituting players. Once you went out, you could not come back in. So, players played both ways and all of the special teams. They only went out if they got hurt! For Johnny, the games were frustrating. Having to just watch and not playing game after game was difficult, but he understood why. His practices became his games. While others didn't like to practice, he did. Johnny found out how much he liked football and how he sometimes wished he had done this before. But what was done was done and he'd enjoy it as long as he could. He would be ready when Coach Johnson called on him.

School had become interesting for him. He liked his government and history classes. He wanted to know why things had happened the way they did in 1929. Reading and listening about "The Great War" and how unions organized and worked really caught his interest. He only had one uneasy situation.

"What's going on Danny?"

Johnny had turned the corner from the long hall in the English wing and found Danny Carey with several of the boys from North Beach around him. Danny and Johnny kinda stood out from the other boys by the way that they dressed and often heard about it. Always dressed in jeans with the cuffs rolled up four or five inches was a dead giveaway that they came from Butchertown.

"What da ya know. Another cow hand from good ole Butchertown. I could smell you as you came around the corner" Aldo Giordano and his two friends laughed out load.

"Look at this one. No hands. You must have a pig for a mother." Aldo pointed at Danny That really pissed Danny off

"Fuck you! You little prick" Johnny laughed out load on that comment!

"Hey Danny, why don't you give Aldo, the prick, a Butchertown welcome and I'll entertain these two."

"Sounds good Johnny"

Danny made short work of Aldo as Johnny went to work on the closest friend of Aldo's. The third North Beach boy took off running down the hall to the outside door when he saw Danny land his right stub to Aldo's face.

"Now Aldo, you should be nice to us Butchertown boys. We just want to get along with everyone. Now you just get along back to class" Johnny said with a smile.

Aldo and his friend Enzio stayed on the floor as Johnny and Danny walked away. Aldo made a gesture to them *"You'll get yours."*

Unfortunately for Johnny, Coach Johnson never called for him to play. He watched all nine games from the sideline and never stepped on the field. His teammates had a great appreciation for him. He worked so hard, and learned so much and was always a positive person in practice and games. He was the only player not to get into a game. Johnny learned some very important and valuable lessons during his time on the team that would follow him during his life. Playing on a team made him a better person. He now knew what it felt like to be the least important person, but still had a place on the team. He would make sure that when he had boys of his own, they would play on organized high school teams. It didn't matter what sport, but they would play. Learning how to be a great teammate was very important to him.

Johnny's last day of school was on a Monday after the last game. He turned in all of his books and thanked all of his teachers. He enjoyed his time as a senior and was glad that he had gone back to school. But now it was time for him to get back to work and back to real life! Not the same for Little Joe. He decided he would finish the school year and spend more time with his new friend, Genny!

By 9:30 am Johnny was at the Teamsters Union Hall looking for work. That first week he picked up a few jobs driving for different outfits. That next Sunday after the 8:00 mass, Johnny talked with Jack Allen about getting back on.

"As soon as we have something open up, I'll let you know. Stay patient and keep going to the union hall for jobs. Things will pick up for us before Christmas."

Jack wanted Johnny back at Allens. There wasn't a job that he couldn't do. The business was changing though. His drivers had to not only be physical, because they had to load and unload their trucks, they had to know about all of the different cuts from all of the animals so that they could sell them! Johnny had been butchering beef, hogs and lambs since he was six and had a great knowledge about the business. He also had a great personality for selling to the store owners. Jack had watched him work the streets building his little newspaper business and knew that he needed Johnny on the trucks doing the same things for Allens.

In the meantime, Johnny got a part time weekend job delivering newspapers for the Call-Bulletin. He was on call for Saturday and Sunday mornings to drop off the papers in different parts of the city to kids for them to sell. Just like he did. This part time work started out as a substitute driver and wouldn't work into a full-time job on the weekends until years later.

On one of the days that he didn't get any work from the union, he ran into his sister Margret downtown. The union hall was close to the Bank of America which is where she worked. They had lunch together and actually had a nice talk about life. Margret's attitude towards her brother had really changed. She saw that he was a hard worker, loyal to his Aunt Lizzy and his reputation of being a tough guy also included being a real good guy. Everyone in Butchertown knew him and liked him.

Chapter Six

Being a senior in high school was exciting for Gina Rosaia. Even though she would not turn 16 until October, she fit right in with the other girls at Saint Bridget's School for Girls. This was her fifth year at the school which had become her home away from home. She was well liked by her classmates. Gina's personality was that of a happy and quiet young lady. She always had nice things to say about others as she did not like confrontation. With the sisters though, she had no problem discussing the topics that they studied in class. There were times that she didn't agree with them and she would let them know that. She excelled at problem solving, organizational skills, arithmetic and reading comprehension. Sister Rose, who was in charge of continuing education, knew that Gina would be successful at the college level and that she had a bright future. The issue would be paying for the education. She would have to attend the new two-year college that was just starting to take students called The City College of San Francisco.

At Saint Bridget's, the sisters required the students to participate in at least one extracurricular activity. It took Adele some time to figure out what she should become involved in. Music was something she enjoyed, but unfortunately singing was not something that she should pursue! Playing an instrument cost too much money and she really wasn't interested in. Gina thought about getting involved with the theater, but she was just too shy for that.

"Gina, with your height and athletic ability's you would be a natural at basketball"

Sister Kathleen was the nun who taught physical education and was also in charge of intramurals at the school. Standing at 5'8, Adele was one of the better athletes at the school and one of the tallest! Sister Kathleen had started teaching all of the girls the new game in their small gym when Gina was a freshman and intramurals counted as an extra activity.

Now a senior, Saint Bridget's girls had a basketball team that played in a league for girls and Gina was on that team. Sister Kathleen was the coach. Girl's athletics at that time was usually an intramural program at many schools. On occasion, for some sports, if there was enough interest, several schools would get together and play a small schedule. No championships, standings or all-star teams would be chosen. This was a great opportunity for the girls of Saint Bridget's and Gina Rosaia.

Girls' basketball in the 1930's was played differently than the boys. It would not change for several decades! Only one girl per team was allowed to play on both sides of the half court line. Two players were designated as offensive players and two were designated as defensive players. Adele usually played on the offensive side of the court. For a tall girl, she possessed a really good two-handed set shot. On occasions the coach allowed her to play the center position, which played both offense and defense.

"Girls, I'm very proud of what you accomplished this year as a basketball team. You won more games than you lost, which is nice! Most importantly, you learned how to work hard together for

a common goal. You found out that everyone had a specific role for our team that helped make us successful. These are important lessons for you to learn and understand as you begin your adult life. Many of you will begin working at jobs where you will need to be a good teammate. Knowing how to find your role and getting along with others for a common goal will also be important"

Sister Kathleen knew that athletics was a great teacher of life skills and that these young ladies will be much better at life as it moved forward because they had the experience of being on a team. It was sad that schools had these opportunities for boys but not for girls.

"Thank you, Sister Kathleen. I'm really happy that you got me to play basketball. It is a fun game! I enjoyed the practices, even the running! The games though, they were really fun. I found out that I enjoyed the winning, and that when we lost, I would get very upset. I don't like to lose! I hope that I can take the life lessons that we learned with me."

Most of Gina's social life was centered around school, some of the parties at the Saint Francis Hotel and Sundays after mass. Those Sundays were the only time that she ever had to interact with boys. As she got older though, most of the boys her age stopped attending the gatherings after mass.

"Marion, how are we supposed to meet any boys if they don't come after mass to the church hall?"

It wasn't like the two girls were boy crazy, but eventually they both wanted to have families. Neither knew many boys older than them, and the ones that were their age were not very interesting.

"Don't worry Gina. Soon you'll be going to college or working. We'll have plenty of opportunities to meet some nice young men."

Marion had already graduated from high school and was working at a department store downtown called Macy's. Marion was almost three years older and was beginning to experience the life of a young woman. She had been on several dates with some of the local North Beach boys and one date with a young man that worked at Macy's.

There were some very nice guys in the North Beach area but life in the old Barbary Coast was becoming a little unsafe. Times were changing. In May of 1932 Luigi Malvese was found dead in the front seat of his no longer shiny black Ford. He was shot several times. Five months later on the last day of October, Genaro Brocollo was gunned down in front of The Hotel D"Colorant on Columbus Ave. in the morning as he was starting his usual walk. No one was charged for either of the two murders. The entire neighborhood knew who was responsible, but there wasn't any actual proof. Most of Brocollo's "men" left San Francisco and headed for Chicago to find work. The few that stayed, gave their allegiance to Frankie "the Hat" Lanza. Frank Lanza had taken control of the illegal distribution of alcohol, drugs and prostitution. He was also the man who ran protection for the local business's along with collecting various loans.

Nunzio Alioto had constructed the first restaurant on the wharf in 1932. He combined his fresh fish stand with a seafood bar specializing in crab and shrimp cocktails. It had become very popular not only with the Italian laborers, but also others from around the city. In early 1933, Nunzio passed away leaving the business to his wife and sons. Also lost was the leadership in the local fishing unions. Eventually, mid 1934, the shipping and fishing unions would strike and close the wharf and other businesses in the city. The ten-day strike and violence and protests that went with it ended in new leadership and new contracts. Frank Lanza was not a part of any unions.

With Genaro Brocollo and Nunzio Alioto no longer in the picture, Frankie "the hat" Lanza was the uncontested leader of the Cosa Nostra.. His reign along with his sons that followed, lasted for almost forty years in the North Beach area.

Although prohibition ended in 1932, Lanza made sure he received his share of the profits from the local restaurants, bars and family stores that sold alcohol. The young men growing up in North Beach had two choices. They could either work on the fishing boats or work for Frank Lanza. Only a few made the choice of working for Lanza. One was a soon to be graduate of Galileo High School named Aldo Giordano and his friend Enzio Tortelli.

Chapter Seven

     In July of 1934, the International Longshoreman's Association, led by Harry Bridges, organized a strike that took a strong hold on San Francisco. On what was called "Bloody Thursday," July 5th, 64 protesters were injured and two died. The funeral that followed, which went through the heart of the City, brought together all unions behind the cause of the Longshoreman. On July 12, the Teamsters of San Francisco meet at Dreamland Auditorium to take a unanimous vote to back Harry Bridges and the Longshoreman. Johnny Turnbull was at that meeting. He saw firsthand, the power of people working together for a common goal. He became a solid union man that day. He had the opportunity to shake hands and talk with Harry Bridges that day as they would remain friends for a long time. After the vote all Teamsters joined the strike the following day, as did all other unions. Nothing left the docks on the wharf until the union settled. More loaded ships were anchored in the bay than all of the abandoned ships left in the old harbor in 1849.

Because of the success of this strike, the following year the United States government passed the Wagner Act. This act created the National Labor Relations Board that protected the rights of workers to organize into unions. This monumental strike and settlement brought economic and political power to labor unions for many years to come.

Things had not been very good for workers, even after the great depression had come to an end. Men were working, but under terrible conditions. This strike made a big difference for all of the butchers in the city as well as the Teamsters that worked in Butchertown.

In 1936, young John Turnbull had just turned 21. He had been driving and delivering for James Allens and Sons for over two years as a full-time employee. His best friend, Joe Dalpagetto, was back working at Allens also, but in what was called "The Pork Room". Kenny Miles, another of the group of four friends finished high school and started working at H. Moffet Company on the "Kill Floor". Danny Cary had just finished up at Galileo High school and was working out of the Butchers Union Hall. He would go to the Hall each morning looking for jobs. Some would last a day or two and some for a week at a time. He was looking to catch on at one of the four remaining slaughter houses in Butchertown.

All four of the friends worked hard, but also played hard. John was still trying to perfect his bull dogging at "the Corral". At least one night a week he would head to the Corral and practice. Saturdays were also a day to practice and get better. He'd see Nellie there riding her horse and roping. Saturday nights they usually got together for a movie or spent time at Cyril DeNikes restaurant.

At this time of life, Johnny had become a very athletic looking well-built young man. He did have a long upper body compared to his shorter legs. He combed his almost black hair down the middle and usually wore a cap tilted just a little, when he was outside. His face had developed the look of a strong-willed guy. He definitely was not pretty but women did like the way he presented himself.

Little Joe was still on the shorter side with a thick beard that he shaved daily to go along with his still dark complexion. The curly hair was still there but it wasn't as thick as it used to be. He also had dark brown eyes that were topped off by one long hairy eye brow. He had developed "Popeye "forearms from butchering for so many years. Kenny had continued to grow as he got older too. He stood an inch taller than Johnny at 6"3. The large frame that he had, supported a portly 237 pounds. He sported average length dirty blonde hair also combed down the middle. His face was not a fat face, but kind of handsome! He did have dark brown eyes that set him apart from most guys. Danny at 18, was still changing in his appearance. He loved his buzz cut for his hair. He also used a little butch wax at the front of his head, just to the side. This gave him an unusual look for the time but it fit his personality. His smile always had just a little smirk. Danny had grown taller than Joe, but would never be six feet. He had what was called the French look. High waste short body. These four young men stood out when they walked together because of how different they were.

Once the spring came around though, most of the weekends for the "boys" would be spent on the road at a rodeo somewhere in the San Joaquin Valley or one of the small towns in the east bay. Johnny was the only one that would enter but the others would come along to watch and for all of the fun that went on at the rodeos.

There were always dances and lots of young women to meet. They drank their fair share of beer and whiskey too! If John was successful, they could get a hotel room for Saturday night. If not, there was always a stable to sleep in along with the animals!

They also discovered that on Saturday nights, somewhere at one of the barns, the cowboys would get together and set up hay ropes for fights. After the fights, they would all go out and party together. A lot of money got exchanged at these fights and the boys did well at picking the winners. A fight usually lasted three to four three-minute rounds or until one fighter quit, got knocked out or stopped by his corner. There wasn't any referee. Just a few rules existed: no biting, no hair pulling. No pokes to the eyes and no punches or kicks to the groin. Anything else was good. Oh, and no gloves or wraps.

"Hey boys I hear we got some good matches going tonight"

Kenny Miles really enjoyed watching the fights. He actually knew something about the art of boxing. He could pick out the good ones and could also pick out the flaws in their approach. Since he knew the fighters, he was able to make the boys some good cash by picking out the winners!

Usually, the Bull Dog event happened on Saturday mornings but at the Salinas Rodeo, it wasn't going to take place until Sunday. When the boys found the barn where the fights were going to happen, Buck the organizer/referee was asking for volunteers to fight. One of the cowboys who was going to fight got hurt earlier in the day riding bulls. This didn't happen all of the time, but every once in a while, someone would get nicked up in the rodeo.

"Hey you!" Buck pointed at Johnny

"You look like someone who could mix it up a little. Na ! You're too skinny"

That kinda pissed Johnny off a little.

"Hey! What's in it for me if I take you up on this?" Johnny was thinking why not find out if it would be worth it. Plus he had never passed up a fight.

"All the beer you can drink at the Cantina downtown after the fights are over" was the reply, as Buck walked towards the prospective fighter.

"Make that all the beer all four of us can drink and you got yourself a deal"

Buck shouted back *"Only if you win! So, if your in, you better get ready then, cause you're up first"*

"Johnny, you're not really going to do this?" Dan Cary knew his friend was a capable guy, but he was a little worried.

"No problem, Danny. That Buck guy pissed me off! Skinny? Maybe be. We'll just have to show these guys what a Butchertown Boy is all about!"

As Johnny pulled his shirt off *"Kenny, you find out who I'm fighting and tell me how to beat him! Joe, we are going to give you ten bucks apiece. That's forty dollars to win on me! We'll make some money and drink for free tonight boys!"*

With that much money on the line, Johnny would make sure he would not quit. And he'd never been knocked out before.

"Alright Johnny my boy. This guy is big but slow. He has a great right hand, so stay to his left or crowd him to his right. Be careful getting in close to him. He keeps his left way too low when he moves. So, move him before you punch with your right. Oh, by the way, he's lost just once before."

"Great. Joe make sure you get some good odds! I'll make sure it goes at least two rounds"
Johnny winked his eye. It probably would take a round or two to get pissed off enough to get after it he thought.

With his shirt off, he did not look skinny any more. He had a well-developed chest and ripples for a stomach. Johnny's biceps and triceps were good size but not huge. What caught most eyes was the size of his back muscles! They came together in a V at the base of his waist just above his butt at the belt line. You knew that he was strong and was a well worked guy.

Well, Johnny was wrong. Ken was right. The big fella hit Johnny with his right as the fight started.

"Shit! Didn't crowd him enough" Johnny thought as he scrambled to his feet, and to get away before he got hit again.

"I told you this would be easy money Jake"

Johnny could hear Buck tell Jake, his opponent.

"Now I'm really pissed. Fuck Buck. I'm gone a kill this guy right now" Johnny was mad at both Jake and Buck!

As Jake came towards him, Johnny made a quick move to his left and then stepped back to his right and let go with his own right hand that landed right on the big guy's jaw. It was timed just right as Jake had his mouth open while trying to say something. A quick left to the nose followed up by another right to the same spot on the jaw and the big guy dropped to one knee. Johnny without thinking, placed his right boot to the bleeding fighters face driving him into the hay bail. Having been in this situation before, Johnny followed him to the bail throwing both hands until Buck pulled him off.

"Fucker. Easy money ha?" Johnny pushed Buck away and gt in his face. *"Next time get me someone who can fight better than that. And it will cost you some real money"* Johnny yelled at Buck. He was still mad and it would take him some time to cool off.

After a minute or two Johnny said to Kenny *"Nice call Kenny. You were right about that right hand"*

"Yeah, but you moved too quick for him. He never moved his left. Your punch just went right over the top of it" Kenny had a good laugh at that.

"Johnny, nice job, I guess! I missed all of it!" *"I hear you got knocked down! First time for a long time"* Little Joe was laughing with a big smile. Johnny laughed to as he shrugged his shoulders.

"Did you get any good odds" Dan asked Joe

"No, it ended too fast. But we did come away with a total of eighty bucks!" Little Joe was really pleased. It only took five minutes. Plus, they would drink a lot of free beer tonight.

While the boys were at The Cantina and drinking the free cold beer, Kenny asked Johnny about him being serious about continuing to step in between the hay ropes at next week's rodeo.

"If that prick Buck offers me enough money. Yeah! We can keep pooling our winnings and make some real money!"

The rest of the summer of 36 and 37 John and the boys continued to attend the small rodeos and have fun doing it. Johnny would only fight guys that Kenny had watched. Fighting was a great way to make extra money and he was good at it. Each of the boys had their part of the business. Little Joe would place and collect the bets; Dan would help Johnny get ready and take care of his needs during the fight and Kenny was the strategist. He'd tell Johnny what he needs to do and look for before and during the contests. It was difficult on Johnny especially after Bull Dogging during the day. He enjoyed that part a whole bunch. The fighting was just for the money. And they had done really well.

The last weekend of every summer would be spent at the beach in Santa Cruz. No rodeo, no fighting, just going to the beach and hopefully enjoying good weather and relaxing at the new amusement park. The evening dances were also fun because the girls were different than what they were used too. No cowgirls and lots of new and pretty faces. The beer and whiskey were good but expensive. At DeNikes, back home, it was a lot cheaper, and a short walk home! But this was vacation!

After the spring and summer rodeo season, Johnny and Little Joe loved to pick out a college football game to go watch on Saturday afternoons. Saint Mary's College, the University of San Francisco and Cal all had really good teams. Coach Pop Warner was beginning to turn around Stanford but both Joe and John really liked the Santa Clara Broncos. Kezar Stadium in Golden Gate Park was a great place to watch and it usually had a full crowd of 55-60 thousand people. It was a great atmosphere and a pint of whiskey in each of their coats made the afternoon, until they could get to DeNikes for a stake, some high balls and an evening of fun.

When football season was over in January, the boys had some great places to go hunting. The south bay along San Bruno Road was great for shooting ducks and geese. They also had a different but great taste if you cooked them up just right. For some reason, Aunt Lizzy loved to prepare the fowl for dinners. She made sure that they came with all of the fifteens. Including mashed potatoes and gravy with plenty of fresh vegetables and fruits. She would always make sure she would enjoy a glass or two of white wine with the dinner. If they were really lucky, they would also enjoy some berry pie and vanilla ice cream.

Chapter Eight

Looking out of the window that is on the second floor of the flat on Kearny Street this cold November morning, told Gina to get out her heavy scarf and coat. The fog was very thick and very wet. The four blocks walk down Kearny to Columbus Ave. and the Bank of America building would normally take twenty-five to thirty minutes. This morning's walk would go much faster! These walks had gotten a little lonely for the eighteen-year-old Italian girl. Her longtime companion, Teddy, made his last walk with her about a year ago. She woke up one morning to find that Teddy had passed away at the foot of her bed that night. She loved that dog so much! He had always been there for her to; talk with and laugh and cry with. They shared everything. She couldn't see there ever being another dog like Teddy.

"Gina, make sure you are covered up this morning. And bring your umbrella just in case"

"I have everything ready Aunt Celia! I'll walk fast this morning!"

"Remember, that tonight we have dinner here with Agnes and Charlie. So, hurry home to help me with dinner."

"I will be right home. No stopping anywhere."

Gina knew that something important was happening tonight. Charlie and Agnes very seldom came by for dinner on a Friday night.

Gina's walk was fast. At five foot eight inches tall, her long legs could cover a lot of ground quickly. She had developed into a very pretty young lady. Her long black hair was always done to perfection. Agnes had taught her how to dress and use very little make up on her face. She sported deep brown eyes and a soft looking mouth. Her nose fit nicely in between with some fine lines. Because she was tall for a woman, she was thin looking. High heels would really bring out the shape of her lower legs.

She actually enjoyed the walk, she was getting used to walking alone and enjoyed the sights, sounds and smells of the streets. Every once in a while, when the wind blew just right, the famous smell of Butchertown would fall among the North Beach families. She had never been to Butchertown, but had heard many stories about it and what went on there. In fact, one of her coworkers was born, raised and lived there.

This morning though, with the fog, there would only be the usual sights and sounds that would blend in as Gina would think about many things on her walk to work.

After finishing one year of school at the City College of San Francisco, Gina had to find a full-time job. The cost of school was way too much for Gina and the family. Charlie Lagomarsino who did all of his banking at the Bank of America, helped Adele get a job at the bank about sixteen months ago. She missed going to school and taking interesting courses. Gina had not decided on a major field of study, she just had taken many introductory classes. The work at the bank was easy but boring!

Gina had also had a chance to meet many interesting and nice students. Several of the young male students had taken an interest in her. It was fun for her to talk with these young men. They were a lot different than the boys she had known from the North Beach area. So far, none of them interested her enough to go on a date with. Aunt Celia probably would not let her go out anyway. Celia wanted Gina to meet a nice Italian boy! She knew most of the boys her age in the area but again, she had no interest in them. There was one though that was very interested in her. And he let everyone know. Aldo Giordano always made sure that he talked with Gina when she walked to work or on her way home. Smoking a cigar and standing in front of The Hotel D'Oloran on Columbus was Aldo Giordano and his friend Enzio. They both had been working for Frank Lanza since they left Galileo High School in 1934. They did little odd jobs for Frankie "The Hat". He had now been working out of the Hotel since Genaro Brocollo was shot and killed. He wanted everyone to know that he was the man now. Adele walked by the hotel every morning on the way to the bank and work.

"Good morning, Miss Rosaia! Can I walk you the rest of the way to the Bank?"

Aldo wore a cheap suit with a tilted hat. He always had a flower pinned to his lapel that was usually a day old. Aldo also smoked a very large cigar and as most Italians made many hand and arm movements when he talked. Every morning, he was extremely nice to Gina.

"No thank you Aldo. You and Enzio there, have way more important things to do" She had a little smile on her face.

Gina could not see herself doing anything with either of the two boys. First off, she was taller than both of them! She didn't care for short men. They were not attractive and she didn't like the fact that they worked for Frank Lanza. These two did have their share of local girlfriends because of who they worked for and they spent a lot of time at the old Bella Union!

"AH, It's not a problem! Aldo replied

Gina waved over her head, smiled and just kept walking.

"Dam Enzio! She's something else. One of these days, she'll give me the time of day"

"No chance, no chance at all Aldo". Enzio said to Aldo

Aldo took a big pull off of his cigar, blew some smoke rings in the air and watched Gina walk away.

Once at work, Gina got started on some of her many little jobs. Most of the people she worked with were very nice, but much older than her. There were four other younger women who worked in the front part of the bank. Gina, did not work with costumers, but in the offices doing paper work, filing and typing. The other women worked in front of the building as tellers. They would take breaks at different times and Gina did have the chance to talk and get to know them.

"You know Gina That I have a younger brother that would be a perfect person for you to meet. He's a hardworking, good man. And he loves to have a good time!"

Margret Turnbull had been working at the bank for several years. She was one of the older women who worked there. Gina didn't know what to think about her. Sometimes she had the attitude that she was better than most of the other girls. You might say a little stuck up. She almost never smiled and never seemed to have fun at work. In fact, Adele was surprised that they were even talking today!

"I should set you two up. It would be easy to do."

The funny part about this, was that Margret had told her brother John Turnbull about this really nice girl at the bank that he should meet. Johnny was not to excited to get involved with a friend of his sister. Over the past five or six years, Margret had grown to respect her brother and finally saw him as an outstanding young man. He could still be a little crude at times, but he was fun.

"Thanks Margret, but my Uncle Henry doesn't let me go out with anyone he doesn't know."

Gina really didn't want to get involved with her brother. If he was anything like her, it would be a poor experience. But she wanted to be polite in her response.

After work that night, Gina hurried home. The weather was much better than the morning. Most of the time when the fog lifted, and the sun came out, San Francisco was a beautiful place. The walk home also had a nice view of the newly built Coit Tower. This new tall white tower stood on the top of Telegraph Hill. The property was once owned by the Coit family. The last remaining Coit passed away in 1929. Lillie Coit left one third of her large estate to the city of San Francisco for civic beautification. The 180-foot-tall art deco tower was completed in October of 1933.

Once in the front door, Gina quickly ran up the two flights of stairs with her shoes in hand. Uncle Henry was smoking one of his best cigars and tasting his homemade wine. Celia was in the kitchen finishing up the cooking.

"Gina, please set the table for all of us. Make sure you set a place for Alfred also!"

Most of the time Alfred would eat dinner out, but his mother was sure he'd be here tonight. She had asked him to be there. Gina always set a place for him any way!

After Charlie and Agnes arrived, Henry made sure everyone had a glass of his homemade red wine, before everyone sat down. Although a little late, Alfred walked thru the back door as everyone was sitting down. Even though he was there, Celia gave him a long stair. Alfred had seen that many times before, but at his age, he just smiled!

"I am sure you are all wondering just a little, why Agnes and I requested that you all joined us for dinner!"

Charlie had a great way of speaking with people and handling important moments. Standing now and holding a glass of wine

"Henry, Celia! Agnes and I would like you to be the first to know along with Alfred and you "chickie" That, you are going to be grandparents!"

Celia, who was sitting next to Agnes reached out and the two shared a big hug and kiss on the cheek. This was way out of character for Celia, but she was overwhelmed with joy. Charlie and Henry shook hands and hugged also. Everyone shared in the excitement following this big announcement with handshakes and hugs. They all drank a lot of wine, including Gina, laughed and sat around the table talking about the future and how the family could help once the child arrived. The two had waited to have a baby, to make sure their business would be able to survive when Agnes had to step away to be a mother. Things at the Saint Francis Hotel florist and the flower shop on Geary Blvd. Were busy and making money. Charlie could afford the extra help now.

Chapter Nine

Sitting in DeNikes Tavern on Friday nights after work listening to Bennie Goodman, Tommy Dorsey, The Andrew Sisters and Glenn Miller, the four Butchertown Boys had their spots along the bar. Danny Cary and Ken Miles where always the first to arrive. They both now worked at H. Offsets and Company which was on the north side of the corner of Third and Evens Ave. They were both working the kill floor. Danny usually worked as a shroud-er, covering the beef with a wet cloth blanket that was used to smooth the fat out and make it look nice. He'd then push the sides of beef into the holding cooler before it was quart-ed and graded. The hog and the lamb kill had him as a shackle r. His strong wrists and forearms helped make up for only having thumb on his right hand. Ken was a hide remover for the beef and lamb kill. His work on the hog kill was difficult. He had to make sure all of the hair was off of the pig's skin. It was dragged on rails through a boiling hot bath to burn the hairs. What didn't get burnt off, Ken had to scrape off with rosin rocks. Work on the kill floor was difficult. The job paid decent money. Each job had a grade of difficulty which determined how much you made. The work that Dan and Ken did pay both of them the same. $145.00 a month. In 1939, that was the average salary that men were making. Meanwhile Joe Dalpagetto, who only went by "Little Joe" to his close friends, was spending his days working for James Allens in the Pork room next to the main building on the east side along Evens Ave. He too made about the same money as Dan and Ken. One of the perches of all of the jobs was that employees could buy their meat at wholesale prices.

Little Joe would show up at Cyril's and sit at the next to last spot at the end of the bar's right side. When Johnny arrived, he had the end spot, or first base as the boys called it. Johnny didn't like strangers to sit next to him!

By now all four young men had their own "machines". The name they used for cars. They all still lived at home and walked to work, but it was a convenience to own their own car. The friends did a lot together, but not everything. Joe had a girlfriend and Dan and Ken were working on it!

Johnny was always the last to arrive at DeNikes. He was driving truck and selling for Allens. He was gone most of the day with different routes. Friday's route took him to the East Bay. The traffic was not good at all. People had stopped using the ferry services which really crowded the new Bay Bridge that was completed in 1936. The lower deck of the bridge was reserved for truck traffic and the inter-urban railway, and it was still packed on Friday afternoons.

"About time Johnny Turnbull!"

Kenny Miles liked to call Johnny by his full name sometimes.

"Yeah, long day. Had to limp back. Coming off the bridge from Oakland, lost sixth gear. Boys are working on it right now. They weren't too happy with me."

Johnny took great pride in his driving abilities. He didn't like break downs. He also took pride in his ability to load his truck. No one was faster and no one helped him load. He didn't need help. Johnny had taught himself how to carry a quarter of beef on each shoulder from the rails, up the ramp and into his truck. Years later in his sixties, he was still able to load a full truck faster than any two young loaders. He was an amazing worker!

"Dan? You get those tickets for Saturdays ball game?"

The San Francisco Seals baseball team, which played in the AAA Pacific Coast League, had a game against the Portland Beavers at Seal Stadium. Butchertown legend, Lefty O'Doul, was the manager for the 1939 Seals. The Butchertown Boys were big fans of Lefty's. And he was a big fan favorite of all of San Francisco Seal followers.

"Yep Little Joe! Got four right behind the dugout. We'll be so close; we can tell Lefty what he needs to be doing"

"Hear that boy? Listen ..." Gene Autry and *"Back in The Saddle Again"* could be heard in the back ground.

Johnny liked several of Gene Autry's songs. DeNikes had a new music box or some called them a jukebox that was always playing music in the tavern part of the building.

"Which reminds me guys, that we got that same house again on Mission Street in Santa Cruz." Johnny had contacted the owner of the house they had rented from in the past, and they had seven days in Santa Cruz to vacation!

"What are the dates for that again?' Dan yelled from the other end of the bar.

"August 7th through the 13th. You guys' better right it down somewhere so you can get that week off from work. I already put in."

"We just gotta figure out who's driven." Ken pointed to Johnny because he had a four-door ford that could make it there and back. Although the others had machines too, none of them would be able to travel that far!

"Sure! No problem. We'll figure out all of that stuff later. Let's get something to eat. I'm starving."

Santa Cruz California was a great place for people of all ages. It was located just north of Monterey Bay. It took over three hours to get there from "The City" of San Francisco. The road from San Jose into the mountains (Hwy 17) was mostly one lane each way. There were many turns in the road making some people car sick! It did have some straight stretches and a few passing lanes.

The long drive for people was well worth it! For starters, The Boardwalk had a great amusement park. The roller coaster ride built in 1924, was huge and considered at the time one of the best in the world. There were rides for kids as well as adults. As with any amusement park that's worth a darn, it had a gigantic Ferris Wheel that had different colored lights for the night time riders. The salt air combined with the smell and taste of the sugar sweet cotton candy had to make you smile. The kiddy train along the Boardwalk was always full of adults too, it was a great way to go from one end to the other. The Boardwalk also had an indoor 73 horse carousel that gave people a chance at the brass ring! If you were lucky enough to grab and collect several of the rings, you won a prize!

Hamburgers, "Coney Island Red Hots, Red Hots a dime" popcorn and peanuts were there to eat, but also added to the aroma and fun.

The main building overlooking the beach contained the other two main attractions other than the beach. "The Plunge" was a huge heated saltwater swimming and diving pool. Each night the 400,000 gallons of seawater was pumped back into the bay and in the morning, the pool would be refilled and reheated. The other attraction was the "Coconut Grove Ballroom" and stages. One stage overlooked the beach for day time concerts and shows. People would sit on the beach under their big umbrellas and on large beach towels and watch and listen. At nights, many of the Big Bands played to packed houses. The swing era was alive and huge at the time. Some of the most famous Bands played in the "Coconut Grove and its Grand Ballroom. Bennie Goodman, Artie Shaw, Tommy Dorsey and Glen Miller all performed there.

Things were also happening in Europe. In early May of 1939, the Germans invaded Czechoslovakia and were planning on their attack on Poland for September. President Roosevelt was promising Americans that the United States would not get involved. Everyone was hoping that America could stay out of it. Many remembered the tremendous loses from World War I and didn't want a repeat of them. The world was tense and it seemed as though the young people of America knew what was in the future and wanted to enjoy life while they still could.

August could not come fast enough for Gina and Marion. The family trip to Santa Cruz seemed to be the high lite of her year. She was still enjoying her monthly visit from her father Pietro, and sometimes her brother Eddy would join them. Eddy was just a great older brother. They always laughed and joked about things. Eddy was tall also, but had light colored hair not dark black like Gina and her sisters. He worked downtown for one of the auto dealers as a mechanic and on some weekends, he did deliveries and worked on the truck for the Rosaia Brothers Florist.

Gina didn't see much of her sisters. Eva was now married. Florence was still living at the Colma farm, but she had a boyfriend that she spent as much time with as she was allowed. Marion, Gina's best friend, lost her mother Selinda in 1937 and was living in the first floor of the flat on Kearny. She continued to work for Macy's Department store downtown. They still spent evenings together after work in Marion's flat and occasionally they would go out on the town together. But not often. Gina still had to get permission from Aunt Celia. There were still the posh events that Charlie and Agnes were part of at the Saint Francis Hotel. Mrs Epstein didn't have any children. When her husband Julius died from a fall out of his girlfriend's apartment window in 1936, she gave Charlie the ownership of both florist shops. He was like the son she never had. And she really liked having Gina with her at events to talk with. Mrs Epstein was hoping to introduce Adele to some nice young men.

"Make sure "chickie" that you have at least the week of August 14th thru the 18th off at the Bank. If you can't get those dates, let me know. We have the house for two weeks, beginning August 7th." Charlie loved the family vacations. He really enjoyed the down time after all of the summer weddings. If he was needed, he could always get back in a day. Charlie was always dressed to the TEE. He loved expensive suits with a tie and white shirt and suspenders It gave him a distinguished look. His hair was thinning and reseeding. Round glasses covered his eyes and a thin light mustache above his lip and light skin, set him apart from most Italians.

"I'm sure I have that week off. I talked with Mr. Scrivner about those dates a month ago. It will be fun for all of us to get away. Marion and I both bought new bathing suits for the beach and hats to go along with them."

The two girls loved the time there. They could go out at nights without the adults. They also loved going to the Coconut Grove and its Grand Ballroom. There would be a great "Big Band" playing that weekend and hopefully all week. Although, Charlie would accompany them at least one night, he too loved the "Big Bands" and dancing with Marion and Gina. He knew how to have a good time! And boy could he dance!

The two young women made a great looking pair when they walked into the Ballroom. Marion was about a head shorter, and was always dressed a little differently than Gina. She was very attractive and would catch any man's eyes. Marion would always be the first one guys would notice. But she was not as pretty as Gina.

The beach and The Boardwalk were just walking distance from the rented home on Laurel Street. Three blocks to Murray Street, which was the main street that ran parallel to The Boardwalk, up three flights of concrete stairs and the fun would begin.

"You know sister"

Marion and Gina often called each other that when talking to each other.

"I'll look for a nice big beach blanket at the store the next few weeks that will match our suits. We are going to look really good!"

"It's going to be so much fun. I have several dresses to wear at the Coconut Grove that Mrs. Epstein gave to me. How about you sister?"

The two young ladies would spend their evenings for several weeks planning wardrobes and all of the other plans that girls make for trips like that!

Chapter Ten

As usual on a Monday morning all of the Butchertown Boys were up and ready to go at 5:30 AM. After finishing up the normal breakfast of; oatmeal, a couple of strips of bacon and a very hot, black cup of coffee, Johnny climbed into his 1933 brown and white Ford and drove to Little Joe's house. While lighting up a non-filtered smoke by using his thumb nail to light the wooden match, Johnny gave his horn a couple of bumps. Little Joe came flying out the front door, and over the rose hedge in the front yard, just like the old single wing tailback that he was.

"I still got it!" Little Joe still had the same old giggle as he quickly sat in the front seat and slapped his friend on the thigh.

"You got everything Joe?"

"Hell yeah. Let's get going!"

Little Joe, Dan and Ken each brought their stuff for the weekend over to Johnnys on Sunday night August 6th 1939. It was what they always did before leaving for the weekend's fun, so this wasn't anything new.

"OK! Just making sure"

After picking up Dan and Ken, the four started out on the fun filled vacation. The newly completed Hwy 101 started with a steep grade through Visitation Valley called "Boneyard Hill" and then down the "Bloody Bayshore" road. The new highway was an upgrade to the old road but it was very accident prone. It lacked a median barrier, which helped cause many serious accidents. People just were not used to driving with that many cars and high speeds. The trip would take the boys past many towns along what was called the U.S. Route 101 Bypass until they reached San Jose. From there, it was the one lane Hwy 17 to Santa Cruz.

By noon, the brown and white Ford motored into Santa Cruz and down Murray Street, which was the main drag. The first piece of business for the guys after unloading the machine was finding their rooms, hitting the head and a visit to the store. They didn't need to worry about the meat part of meals because they brought it with them. Bacon for breakfast, sausages and hot dogs for lunches and various cuts of lamb, pork and beef, including "hangers" for dinners. What they needed was coffee, smokes, potatoes and odds and ends that go along with the lunches. They had also loaded up at home with beer and whiskey that they could get cheap through Cyril DeNikes Tavern.

It didn't take long and they were swimming in the cold Pacific Ocean. The weather was a nice warm 78 degrees and NO wind. Perfect for the afternoon.

The walk to the beach from their Mission Street home was about twenty minutes. They walked down a curvy Laurel Street for about a mile and a half before it straightened out. From there a short walk of five blocks to Murray Street, then up three flights of stairs to The Boardwalk. They would make this trip every morning to the beach and then again at nights to the Coconut Grove to listen to Stan Kenton and his Band in the main ballroom.

The days at The Boardwalk were full of a lot of fun and excitement. They made sure they hit every ride including the new "Speed Boat" ride into the bay on the "Miss Stagnaro." The dual motored boat held ten passengers as well as the driver. It was a twenty-minute ride along the beach and into the choppy waves of the bay at speeds of 50 to 60 miles an hour.

When the skies became overcast, it was into "The Plunge" for swimming and diving off of the three-meter diving board. The guys weren't the best divers. Lots of big splashes and an occasional belly flop after a missed flip! The afternoon concerts and shows from the stage were enjoyable and relaxing. The guys had been working hard and the time away from the grind was just what "the doctor ordered". They might be a little physically tired when the week was over, but mentally they'd be refreshed and ready to get back to their real life.

"I don't think I could do this forever, but it sure is nice for now"

Dan reached into the ice chest for a cold "Burgie".

"Let me have the honors Dan my boy"

Dan tossed the 12 oz can of beer to Ken. With his opener, he punched two holes at the top of the tin can on one side followed by one hole on the other end. This way the beer would flow faster through the two holes. When the boys started to really have fun they would "shoot" a beer. To "shoot" a beer you had to punch a hole in the bottom of the can, put your thumb over it and then punch two holes in the top of the can. Turn it upside down and let your thumb off of the can. The gravity would help the beer come pouring out at a fast rate! But they usually don't get to that until the afternoon!

"Yes, er e Johnny. This has been a great week" Little Joe laughed. *"Great food, great times and great friends".*

Johnny raised his can towards his friends *"Too next year".*

Monday morning on the 7th of August, Gina watched the flat on Kearny Street awake to a lot of excitement. Aunt Celia was up much earlier than usual. Gina and Alfred had a quite breakfast, as he was out the door at 6:00 am. Gina would be leaving at 7:30 for her walk to The Bank of America. Charlie and Agnes would arrive after she left, to pick up Celia and Henry for the drive south. Charlie drove a brand new 1939 Chevy with four doors. They both opened from the middle. The Green three speed had large white wall tires on the front and back with a big chrome cow catcher radiator on the front. They would stop in San Jose for a long lunch before they hit the road to Santa Cruz. Charlie would drive slowly with the older couple and a pregnant wife. Instead of taking the new highway, they would travel along the old route called The El Camino Real. The woman enjoyed all of the little towns along the way and just in case they needed to stop for something;

bathroom, shopping or just stretching out the legs, it would be easier along that road. Not only were they not used to sitting that long, the car was not all that comfortable!

Once at Laurel Street in Santa Cruz, the small group unloaded the car, got situated and the ladies went to separate rooms to take a nap. Charlie and Henry sat on the front porch in two really comfortable chairs and drank Henry's wine, smoked some fine cigars and talked about life. The two men got along well. Even though there was a difference in age and background, they laughed a lot and shared stories. Both men needed time off away from the city and the city life. The drive from San Jose reminded Henry of his early life in Verpiano Italy. The mountain country side was very similar.

They also talked about life in Italy now and how things would be under the leadership of Benito Mussolini. Italian forces had invaded Albania earlier in the year and they also had signed a treaty with Nazi Germany. Most of the able body males had been brought into the Italian army. Henry had not heard from his brother but, he just figured he too was in the service of El Duce. He was upset at these developments, and thought-out load how he wished his brother and sister had joined him in America. But that didn't happen and it would not.

Gina and Marion's week went very slowly in anticipation for Friday. They made sure everything was ready on Thursday night for the drive Friday after work. Charlie would pick them up after he stopped in at the two florist shops. He felt he could not be away for too many days.

"Girls ready to go?"

With a big smile on both of their faces and all of their bags at their feet.

"Not really"

With big laughs, the girls grabbed their things and headed down the stairs to Charlies 1939 Green Chevy that cost him just over $700.00. For this drive, Charlie took the bypass! They did stop at a rest area on Hwy 17 so that Charlie could eat a sandwich and the girls could visit a bathroom.

It was still light out as the threesome pulled into the driveway on Laurel Street. Henry, Celia and Agnes were all sitting on the front porch enjoying the breeze from the Pacific Ocean that cooled off the night. There had been a steady stream of foot traffic each morning and night of people walking to and from The Boardwalk. Everyone was very friendly to each other, waving, talking and lots of smiles. It was the same groups of people, mostly young, that walked by and sometimes stopped and chatted. One of the funniest was a group of four young men. In the mornings they carried two ice chests and in the early evenings they were dressed up nicely for the night at the Coconut Grove. They always stopped and said hello, especially in the evenings. Celia, at first didn't say much to them, but by Friday, she warmed up. She smiled and even yelled at the men as they walked by. On this night they had already been by.

The family all sat down for a late dinner of pasta, eggplant fried in olive oil, garlic and onions, along with sourdough bread and wine. The girls were a little tired from the long day of work and the drive. Having to sleep in the same room wasn't a problem as both went down early so that they could be ready for the beach on Saturday.

When the morning arrived, it was accompanied by fog that would not burn off until later in the day.

"Let's just walk over to The Boardwalk anyway Marion. I just love the ocean"

Anytime Gina had a chance, she loved to go to the beach in the city and watch the waves roll in and out. It was even better when it was storming. The ocean was so powerful and impressive.

"Sure! Why not! We can see what's new for rides and who's playing tonight at the Coconut Grove Ballroom. I'm sure whomever it is will be here all week."

For some reason Marion was extra excited about going out on Saturday night. Gina just thought they had all week and it wasn't all that important to her. But she would go along and try to have some fun.

"Hey I hope they still have that kiddy train. We can ride on that this morning too!"

Chapter Elven

"Well.... last night boys. Let's make it our best. Let's get over there early tonight and have dinner. We're almost all out of food anyway."

"Good idea Ken. We'll clean out the ice box, have a few high balls and take our time on the walk" Dan answered.

"We might as well clean these places up too. I don't want to do it in the morning before we leave."

Johnny and Little Joe both agreed. *"We can take our time getting things done today and skip the afternoon at the beach. It's overcast anyway."*

Little Joe added *"I think we are all a little worn out! But it has been what we wanted. For me anyway"*

Four o'clock rolled around and the house looked good. They made sure last year that they left the place really clean and they wanted to do it again this year. It made it easier to re rent! And they wanted to be back again. With no more food left in the house and enough drink for a couple of high balls, the boys finished packing what was left in the truck of Johnny's Ford. A change of clothes in the morning and they'd be ready for a quick exit. The coffee shop on the main road would be open early for a fast breakfast and some hot "mud" for the ride home.

As the four men walked down Laurel Street heading to The Boardwalk, they passed the house were the two couples usually sat enjoying the day.

"You boys are a little early tonight" The older of the two women yelled. Celia wore a full-length brown dress that covered her rather round figure. Her graying hair was up in a bun and she wore round glasses that set off her small smile... Her sister, also was in a full-length dress that had more color to it. She was probably the younger of the two women because she had black hair with only a few streaks of gray and not as large.

"Yes Mam! No more food in the house! Going for an early dinner. Last night in town" Johnny had a big smile on his face as he waved and finished with

"You need to join us tonight. Kick up your heels a little. I'll be looking for you!

The two older men looked like they would love too. They each took a long pull off of their cigars and waved along with the two women.

"Thanks for the invite. We just might make it tonight!" They said as they waved.

In the kitchen of the house Marion and Gina could hear the conversation going on outside as they were finishing up tonight's dinner.

"Does The Band start tonight at 8:00 or 9:00?

Marion wasn't sure. They had walked The Boardwalk earlier and read the times on the reader board for the upcoming week. But there were different times for the different nights.

"9:00 tonight sister. So, we have plenty of time. We should get there a little early though. It might be difficult getting a table"

Adele was not going to stand the whole night.

After dinner at the little restaurant in the main building, the guys headed outside for last time on The Boardwalk and some fun. Throwing oversized balls at wooden milk jugs, shooting water through rifles at targets, trying to ring the bell with the sledge hammer and of course one last ride on "The Miss Stagnaro" and the lighted Ferris Wheel had to get done one last time!

It was close to 8:00, so the guys headed to the Coconut Grove Ballroom. Thinking that on a Saturday night with Stan Kenton's Big Band playing, it might get a little crowded. Positioning at the Coconut Grove was important! They needed to have a table that had a clear view of the entry way and the dance floor. Not to mention easy access to the bar. After five nights of being there, they knew just where they needed to be!

For the two sisters the short walk to The Boardwalk seemed to take forever! They got out of the house on Laurel Street a lot later than they wanted to. The good thing though was the weather. The wind had settled down, so there were no worries about their hair getting messed up! The smell of the Pacific Ocean always had a calming effect. The light sweaters that they put on, went well with the dresses that they had on, and they felt pretty good about the way that they looked.

The difficult part about walking into the Coconut Grove was making an entrance! Being a little late, they most likely would not find a table up front and they would have to circle around to the back of the ballroom.

As they got close to the main entrance you could hear The Band playing "Tuxedo Junction". To their surprise, the room was not full yet. Maybe by 10:00 or 10:30 more people would arrive.

"Hey Marion ... Right here"

Gina pointed to an open table that was fairly close to the dance floor and to the entry way.

"Oh perfect. This will be great!"

Just after they sat down and got their sweaters off and, on a chair, two young sailors asked both to dance to "Summer time".

Gina thought that was quick and off they went.

"Holy shit Joe! Check that out!"

Johnny had grabbed Little Joe by the arm and nodded at Gina as she walked towards them to the dance floor.

"Wow! No chance baddie."

Little Joe laughed knowing that Johnny didn't hear a word he said. Women didn't do that to him. He never, ever had singled out some one before. It was usually Joe doing the pointing. Little Joe continued to giggle as Johnny stared at the couple as they walked to the dance floor. The tune seemed to last forever in Johnny's mind. He thought about "cutting in" but that would not be the right thing to do.

Marion and Gina thanked the two sailors and they worked their way back to their table. The Band quickly started to play the new hit by The Glenn Miller Band "In the Mood". Johnny took a deep breath and stepped in front of this tall thin beauty! As he looked into her face and dark brown eyes, she also caught his eyes with hers. After what seemed a long pause, Johnny pointed to the dance floor and smiled.

Gina was really taken by the wonderful look of this man's eyes and the smile. He seems so friendly and he was Tall! She had to look up at him! The music was nice but they both danced as though there was no one else there! His grip was strong but at the same time comforting. And neither one could take their eyes off each others eyes. They moved together at a perfect pace. Not too fast and not too slow.

Johnny was hoping that he would not stumble or step on this girl's feet. He had been known to do that! The feel of her hand in his and his other hand around her back was something that he never felt before. Most girls caused him to bend over because they were so short. In the three minutes or so on the dance floor both had many of the same thoughts; "Don't mess this up", Is this person for real?" and "What do I do when the music stops?"

The tune unfortunately came to an end and they both would have to say something! But, the next tune "It's the way you do it" broke out. Without thinking, Johnny continued to hold Gina's hand and walked her to her table. He pulled out her chair watched her sit down and then he grabbed a chair and sat also.

Facing her *"Hello ...! My name is John. Can I ask you for your name?"*

Gina was very pleased that this young good-looking man named John took the initiative with the conversation.

"Sure" With a smile on her face. *"John, my name is Gina. Gina Rosaia from North Beach in San*

Francisco".

The two continued to chat for the next two or three dances. It was very evident to both, that the surroundings were loud and too crowded. Marion had since joined the two at the table and Gina had introduced John to her. They talked briefly, so as not to be impolite, and John said to Gina.

"How would you like to go outside for a bit and walk The Boardwalk? It's a little loud in here"

"I'd love too"

"Marion ..! We are going outside for a while and we'll be right back"

Gina grabbed her sweater and off they went. As they walked out of the main building, the lights hit the beach just right. The shine of the light hitting the rolling waves was in Gina's mind the perfect sight. They came to a bench along the main walk way and sat down. Many people were walking up and down The Boardwalk and riding the kiddy train but in the next three hours John and Gina didn't notice anyone. They sat and talked the whole time about what they did, where they grew up and a little about family. Every once in a while, the sounds of the ocean and the cool breeze that it provided became noticeable when there were pauses in conversation. As it became chilly, John helped Gina put her sweater on.

Gina was just so at ease. She talked so much more than she ever had to anyone, and laughed, giggled and blush at times. Time passed so fast. Probably the biggest laugh of the night was when they discovered that Margret Turnbull was John's sister that worked with her at the Bank. She had been trying to set them up for a date for a while, but neither one of them wanted to take her up on it! She wasn't too excited about going out with her brother and he was not sure about her nice friend at the Bank!

Before they knew it, Marion was standing in front of the two of them. Hands on hips shaking her head

"Back soon ha!" as she laughed.

"John, right?"

"Yes" he answered as he stood up

"Your friends inside are a little worried about you! They said you've never done this before"

"Ah, ... well yes. Gina and I just got to talking and time flew by. Can I walk you two homes?"

The walk to the Laurel Street home was too fast for both John and Gina. They held hands the whole way, both wishing that it was a longer walk. Upon arriving at the front porch, Marion said her good-byes to both John and Gina.

Gina wanting to continue talking with John asked

"John, would you like a glass of water?"

"Sure" Wow he thought. I can stay a little longer with her.

After about a half an hour, Little Joe, Ken and Dan came walking by. John introduced all three to Gina. The five talked for a bit

"Hey guys, I'll be along in a bit. Don't wait up for me"

The guys took the hint. As they walked off, John sat down again.

"Don't forget, we're leaving at sun up in the morning" Little Joe giggled as the three walked away.

The two new friends spent the next several hours just talking and getting to know each other even better. They exchanged phone numbers and set up a date for the next weekend after Gina returned home. The sun was just starting to come up when John was forced to say his good-bye's. Standing on the front porch holding both of her hands, John squeezed them lightly, turned and walked away.

Needless to say, Gina would not get any sleep. As she walked into her room, Marion perked up from her bed and the two talked about what had just happened that night! The excited Gina talked until it was breakfast time.

Charlie was the first to come into the kitchen, where the girls were sitting at the table.

"You two have a good time last night? Oh, and how was the Band?

Marion was quick to reply, as Gina was chewing on a piece of bread with her egg.

"Interesting. You could say very interesting. We meet some very interesting people. The Band? Gina what did you think of the Band?"

With a big smile on her face and a chuckle to go along with-it Gina said *"Loud. Very loud, I could barely hear my own self talk."*

The conversation continued without any hints of Gina's new friend. After going to the 10:30 mass at the Holy Cross Catholic Church, which just happened to be off Mission Street and walking distance, Gina took a nap!

Johnny arrived just before the rest of the guys were getting up. The guys had no idea he had stayed up all night. They thought that he was just up before them. They loaded the machine and headed to the coffee shop. Johnny drank several cups of the black hot coffee and bought a large one to go. He was still excited about last night and meeting Gina. Unlike the two girls, they didn't talk too much. The guys settled into the car for the ride home and slept the whole way. With a "Lucky Strike" hanging from the left side of his mouth and the cup of coffee between his legs, Johnny shifted into first gear and away they went. Thinking about his new friend, driving the curves, down shifting and spilling the coffee easily kept him awake and alert. He did have to pull over before he got to the highway! He had drunk a lot of coffee! With no, rest stop around, he found a tree and some bushes for relief.

Chapter Twelve

Beginning on the Monday night after her week in Santa Cruz, John and Gina talked on the phone for four consecutive nights. A nice card and a flower arrangement from Charlie's shop on Geary Blvd greeted Gina and the group when they arrived home on that Sunday evening.

Aunt Celia and Uncle Henry were taken by surprise with the flowers and card that were for Gina. That evening after dinner the three sat at the dinner table as she told the older couple about her first night at the Coconut Grove Ballroom and her new friend. She also let them know that she wanted to continue to see him and that they had made plans to go on a date that next Friday evening after work. Celia was not very happy about the two dating. After all, the young man was Irish and from Butchertown!

Celia's first test for the Irish boy came on the first date. John buzzed the door at the base of the flat on Kearny. Celia opened the window, which was three floors up and dumped a bucket full of boiling water at John. It was a good thing he herd the window open. The water missed him...

Celia yelled own at John something in Italian that he could not understand. She was very angry looking and hoping he would leave.

"Thank you for the greeting. Very unusual"! John smiled and waved. *"I can't wait to meet you. Gina has told me much about you"*

It didn't take long for John to win over acceptance of Celia and Henry. His smile, along with his fun demeanor and wit certainly helped things. They recognized him from Santa Cruz and how nice he was in front of the house. Also, the fact that he was Catholic and was taking Gina to Sundays mass didn't hurt.

Right from the start of their relationship, John and Gina both knew that they were meant for each other. Through their many long talks, they found out that they had much in common. The most common element was their want and need to be a part of a complete family.

The weekend after Thanksgiving of 1940, John and Gina were married. Little Joe was John's Best Man and Marion the Maid of Honor for Gina. They settled in the Bayview area of San Francisco, which was close to where John grew up. Joe also bought a home in the same neighborhood, just a few blocks away with his new family. By 1955, the Turnbull family had six members living a small house on the side of a hill. Life changed when they were encouraged to sell their home by a new local group called the "Black Panthers." With the money that they made from selling their home, they built a new home in a brand-new neighborhood down the peninsula in the town of San Bruno. The home sat bordering the huge San Bruno Park...

Gina is very tired now. As she prays to Jesus tonight, she asks him if it would be ok if tonight she could fall asleep and dream of the times she had spent with John. The next thing she sees is John walking towards her with that big smile of his. She feels so good! It's been forever since she felt this good. They hug and kiss each other.

The next morning Janet, the very nice young lady came in to wake Gina up. Gina just looked so happy. She had a smile on her face. The young lady shook Gina very lightly, but she didn't wake up.

www.ingramcontent.com/pod-product-compliance
Lightning Source LLC
Chambersburg PA
CBHW080855120626
46553CB00009B/2635